AS I HAVE LOVED YOU

First Edition

© 2024 by Alemayehu Desta. All rights reserved.

Printed in the United States of America
ISBN: 9798326750914

Imprint: Independently published
First Self-Published in June 2024
Front cover design by Basleal Senbeto
Senbetobasleal@gmail.com

Alemayehu Desta
Alemayehudesta@msn.com

Dedication

This book is dedicated to:

The thirty-four martyrs of the Ethiopian Orthodox Tewahedo Church in April of 2015 in Libya

The twenty-one martyrs of the Coptic Orthodox Church in February of 2015 in Libya

The thousands of Ethiopian Martyrs, priests, deacons and the faithful, killed in the last six years because of their faith in Christ and their love for Christ
And to their survivors who are living with the painful memory of the horror they have witnessed!

Table of Contents

Preface 4

Introduction 6

Chapter 1 God's Love before Creation 9

Chapter 2 God's love in Creation 14

   I.   Creating man with His own hands and giving Him the breath of life 14

   II. Creating man knowing that he would sin .. 15

   III. Creating man last on the sixth day of creation. 17

   IV. Creating man in His own image and likeness. 20

   V.   God's deliberation before creating man. ... 25

   VI. Making Eve from Adam's ribs 27

   VII.   The Tree of Knowledge 29

Chapter 3 God's love after the fall 37

Chapter 4 God's love after the promise of salvation 45

   I.   The Covenant of Noah 46

   II. The Covenant of Melchizedek 49

   III. The Covenant of Abraham 50

   IV. The Covenant of Moses 52

V. The Covenant of David 54

Chapter 5 God's love in the fulfillment of His promise 57

Chapter 6 God's love in the suffering and Crucifixion of His Son 61

  I. His death on the Cross 62

  II. His Resurrection 66

  III. His Ascension 74

Chapter 7 God's Love in the Sacraments 78

  I. Baptism 78

  II. Confirmation 82

  III. Holy Communion 84

  IV. Priesthood 87

  V. Repentance (Confession) 91

  VI. Matrimony 95

  VII. Unction of the Sick 97

Chapter 8 God's love in His Teachings 99

Conclusion 103

Preface

How much does God love us? This was a question of personal contemplation that started with a short article I wrote about love for a local church publication. Contemplation of God's love is like getting into an ocean one cannot swim out of. King David, who has experienced both the wrath of God and His infinite merciful love, in contemplation of such love asked, "What is man that you are mindful of Him...?"

It is impossible to get an absolute answer to King David's question. Because to answer it, one must be able to fathom the magnitude and the measure of God's love. But, as God is unfathomable, so is His love. We can only try to understand how His love is manifested in our lives from the beginning of creation. As our knowledge of God comes from His self-revelation, our knowledge of His love also comes from the self-revelation of His goodness, kindness, righteousness, graciousness, benevolence... Why is man created last? Why in a unique manner? Why in the image and likeness of God? Why did God have to give His only begotten Son for us? Why did He have to suffer, carry our burden and be chastised on our behalf?

Contemplating on these questions helps one grow in in the knowledge of God's love. This book is written from a personal contemplation and desire to grow in the knowledge of His love – a love that is beyond our mind, and our imagination to fully understand and grasp; but a love that is as visible as the morning sun;

a love that can be felt as the touch of a soothing hand; a love that captivates the mind; a love that burns the heart as the travelers of Emmaus */Luke 24:32/;* a love that endures forever and a love that is ultimately manifested on the Cross. There are no words that can express this love and to measure its magnitude. It feels dreadful to write about the love of God that surpasses all knowledge, but the desire to put my personal contemplation into words is too great to be restrained. Through this writing, it is my hope and prayer to grow in grace of the love of God, and for the readers to partake in the grace of His Love – which is integral to His essence.

Introduction

Love is something people define in many ways. But it is a novel virtue that is not simple to explain, understand or to live by. It is the most essential virtue preached by many religious institutions, but it is probably the least practiced. Its value in Christianity is characterized in the words of St. Paul: *"Now abide faith, hope and love, these three; but the greatest of these is love."* /1 Cor. 13:13/.

Love is an attribute of the essence of our God: *"God is Love!"* /1 John 4:8/ It is given to us to live by it and to live in its grace: *"Beloved, if God so loved us, we ought also to love one another."* /1 John 4:11/. It is therefore through understanding this essential attribute of God that we can truly understand what love is. It is when we understand how much the Lord God loves us, that we can begin to truly understand what love is. That is why, when the Lord Jesus Christ gave his disciples a commandment of love, He said: *"This is my commandment, that you love one another as I have loved you."/ John 15:12/*

What we can understand from this commandment is that true love is not loving others according to our own notion of love, but rather loving others according to how our Lord and Savior Jesus Christ loved us. This is exemplified by these words of God: *"For my thoughts are not your thoughts, neither are your ways my ways, says the LORD. For as the heavens are higher than the earth, so are my ways higher than your ways, and my thoughts than your thoughts." /Is. 55:8-9/.* Therefore, we need to diligently seek to understand how He loved us. St Paul reminds us about the importance of understanding the love of God in these words: *"... that Christ may dwell in your hearts through faith, that you, being rooted and grounded in love, may be able to comprehend with all the saints what is the width and length and depth and height – to know the love of Christ which passes knowledge, that you may be filled with the fullness of God." /Eph. 3:17-19/.* We can see from his words that we should be diligent in seeking to understand the love of God, so that we can be *"filled with the fulness of God."*

God in his essence is unsearchable. St. John the apostle said, *"God is love." /1 John 4:8/* Since God is unsearchable in His essence; His love is also beyond the limit of our understanding. That is why St. Paul said that the width and length and depth and height of Christ's love surpasses all knowledge. But we know the Lord God according to how He revealed himself to us, and we can also understand His love according to how He manifested His abundant love for us. As St. Paul said, we must be diligent to know His love, *"to be strengthened with might through the Holy Spirit..." /Eph. 3:16/*

Therefore, to understand His love by His grace, we ask, "How much does God love us? How did He manifest His love for us?" Love is not something that can just be expressed in words but must be manifest in deeds. We should therefore try to understand how God manifested His love from the beginning of creation.

To understand the mystery of Godliness is to grow in the knowledge of the love of God. And it is when we grow in the knowledge of the love of God that it can be reflected in us – in extending the same love to others. That is why St. John wrote: *"Beloved, let us love one another, for love is of God; and everyone that loves is born of God, and knows God. He that loves not knows not God, for God is love."/1 John 4:7-8/*. With this, we will proceed to see how God's love is manifest for us from the beginning of creation.

Chapter 1

God's Love before Creation

"He has chosen us in Him before the foundation of the world, that we should be holy and without blame before Him in love: having predestinated us unto the adoption of children by Jesus Christ to Himself."
Eph. 1:4-5

God is the only uncreated being, and the creator, who has begotten all of creation from non-existence. The intricate nature and the inexplicable order of creation speaks of a meticulous Creator. It is clear that we are not created simply because God is able to create. There has to be a reason and a purpose. Thus, the God who created us must be a God or reason and purpose. That is what we understand from the manner of creation according to Genesis. Moses wrote, *"In the beginning God created the heaven and the earth." /Gen. 1:1/*. These are the foundations of creation. There is no creation that exists outside of these foundations of creation. The story of creation that follows these foundations manifest a plan, a purpose and a reason – that creation is not a spontaneous act of God's might, but a consequence of God's preexisting love.

It is because of His love for creation, and especially for mankind, that He created the world. That is why He planned to prepare a kingdom for our inheritance before He created the heavens and the earth. We can understand this from the words of the Gospel according to Matthew: *"Come you blessed of My Father, inherit the kingdom prepared for you **before** the foundation of the world." /Matt 25:34/*. Commenting on this verse, St. John Chrysostom said, *"He (the Lord Jesus Christ) reveals how great is his bond of love for them (the righteous that will stand on his right when He comes for judgment) and has been from the beginning."*[1]

The kingdom He prepared for us was created on the first day when the heavens and the earth were created: *"In the beginning God created the heaven and the earth." /Gen. 1:1/* But, as stated before, creation is not a consequence of His might, but rather effected by reason and purpose. It is to remind us that He planned to prepare a kingdom for us before He started bringing forth creation that it is written as if this kingdom was *"prepared ... before the foundation of the world."* As St. Basil the Great wrote, *"...the world was not conceived by chance and*

---

[1] John Chrysostom on Matthew 25:34 - Catena Bible & Commentaries. (n.d.). Catena Bible & Commentaries.

without reason, but for a useful end and for the great advantage of all beings..."[2]

The Love of God for mankind even before creation is evident in these words of St. Paul: *"According as He has chosen us in Him **before the foundation of the world**, that we should be holy and without blame before Him in love: having predestinated us unto the adoption of children by Jesus Christ to Himself." /Eph. 1:4-5/.* God in his infinite wisdom and foreknowledge, has determined to send His Son into the world, *"that the world through him might be saved." /John 3:17/.* Knowing man would fall and lose the precious grace of childhood, He *"predestined us unto the adoption of children by Jesus Christ to Himself."*

We are adopted as children again through baptism. St. Paul wrote to his disciple Timothy, *"Who has saved us, and called us with a holy calling, not according to our works, but according to his own purpose and grace, which was given us in Christ Jesus before the world began, But is now made manifest by the appearing of our Savior Jesus Christ, who has abolished death, and has brought life and immortality to light through the gospel. /2 Tim. 1:9/.* It is therefore clear that grace through the sacraments was in God's plan of our salvation, even before the creation of the world. Commenting

---

[2] CHURCH FATHERS: On the Making of Man (ST. Gregory of Nyssa). (n.d.). https://www.newadvent.org/fathers/2914.htm

on these words of St. Paul, St. Athanasius wrote, *"For the grace which came to us from the Savior appeared, as the apostle says, just now, and has come when He sojourned among us. Yet this grace has been prepared even before we came into being.... The God of all then created us by his own Word, and knowing our destinies better than we, God foresaw that even though we were made "good," we should be transgressors of the commandment and be thrust out of paradise for disobedience. Being loving and kind, He prepared beforehand in his own Word, by whom also he created us, the economy of our salvation."*[3]

These words of the Scripture and the holy fathers clearly show that the Lord God loved us even before creation. We are not creations of just God's might, but of His love. This preexisting love is reflected in creation and throughout the history of mankind – from the inception of creation and first gift of life to the ultimate act of love – which is giving one's life for another. /John 15:13/.

Creation is a consequence of God's love. This is manifested not just in the act of creation, but in its perpetual existence. If creation was not the consequence of God's love, there would be no reason to cause its perpetual existence. His preexisting love is what binds creation to the Creator Himself. It is a

---

[3] Athanasius The Apostolic on 2 Timothy 1:9 - Catena Bible & Commentaries. (n.d.). Catena Bible & Commentaries.

persistent love that is not conditioned on anything external to His divine essence. That is why the love that existed before creation persists despite the deeds of created beings – and therefore this is the reason for the perpetual existence of creation.

God's love is eternal, and so is His purpose for creation. That is why St. Paul wrote, *"... And to make all men see what is the plan of the mystery, which from the beginning of the ages has been hid in God... According to the eternal purpose which He purposed in Christ Jesus our Lord. /Eph. 3:9-11/*

The love of God manifested from the beginning of creation therefore is a love that existed even before creation, and as already discussed, a love that is the cause of creation.

Chapter 2

God's love in Creation

I. Creating man with His own hands and giving Him the breath of life

"And the LORD God formed man of the dust of the ground and breathed into his nostrils the breath of life; and man became a living soul." /Gen. 2:7/

The way the Lord God created man is also another manifestation of His love for mankind. He brought forth creation in three distinct ways. There are some He created just with his willful thought or gesture, others by speaking of them to come into existence, and only one He formed with His own hands –man.

He could have created man in the same manner as all other creation, but man was not like any other creation for God. He was an image of Himself – a creation, as intimate with Him as a child with his mother. So, man would not be the work of just His will or His words, but the work of His hands. He also breathed into him the breath of life /Gen. 2:7/.

This is significant in the story of creation because no other details are given about the creation of other creatures. But the creation of man is described in more detail: It details about how God planned to create Him – in His own image and likeness; how He formed Him with His own hands; how He made them man and woman; and about the commandments He gave man – to rule over everything on earth, to be fruitful and multiply and to eat from everything that grows from the earth except from the Tree of Knowledge. All these shows how man is especially dear to the Lord God among all His creation.

The Lord God does not have physical or tangible body as we do, for He is Spirit. "The hand of God" is an expression of His love. And we see this love manifested in the hands of the incarnate Son of God: *"He touched her hand and the fever left her." /Matt. 8:5/;* *"And Jesus moved with compassion, put forth his hand, and touched him, and said... be though clean." /Mark 1:41/;* *"After that he put His hands again upon his eyes and made him look up; and he was restored and saw every man clearly." /Mark 8:25/;* *"And He laid His hands on her, and immediately she was made straight, and glorified God." /Luke 13:13/.* The hand of God formed man from the ground, but the hand of man took the forbidden fruit in rebellion.

II. Creating man knowing that he would sin.

Some people ask about why God created Adam and Eve, knowing that they would sin – since God in His essence is omniscient. If we look at it objectively, this in fact is a manifestation and an act of love. We can understand this with an example of a woman who had conceived a child, though it may be an imperfect example. If the Lord God had decided not to create man because of His foreknowledge that man would rebel against Him, it would have been just as a woman terminating the life of a fetus in her womb. Once man was conceived in the mind of God, He would not deny him the gift of life, because God in His essence in perfectly loving. Therefore, this in fact is a manifestation of His infinite love – that He loved to create man despite His foreknowledge that man would sin against Him. A loving woman who might have whatever negative foreknowledge about a child she conceived, would proceed to bring the child into this world, because her love for the unborn child would compel her to give the child a chance, instead of denying him/her life, because of her foreknowledge. Likewise, since God is love, it would have been against His essence to abandon His plan to create man because of His foreknowledge that man would sin against Him. God's knowledge, before creation, about the fall of man in no way indicates that God predestined the fall of man. But as we have seen in the words of St. Paul, He did predestine to give His only begotten Son for us.

Once God had planned to create man, he was no more a thought but a living being in the realm of His divine existence. God would have to be void of love, or imperfect in His love, to deny man the chance to come into this world and exercise his free will to choose his destiny. And the destiny, without the loving intention of God would have been descent into eternal corruption. But, because of his divine love, He *"predestined us unto the adoption of children by Jesus Christ to Himself." /Eph. 1:5/*. He created man knowing that He would have to give His only begotten Son, that through Him the world might be saved.

III. Creating man last on the sixth day of creation.

The scripture tells us that God created the world and everything in it in six days – and that man was created last of all creation. Why is man, the only one created in His image, created last?

God could create the six days of creation in one moment. If He had done that, creation would be simply taken as a consequence of His will and His might. But He does not do anything spontaneously, without reason. To show us that He is a rational God and that He does everything with reason and purpose, He created everything in six days, confirming daily that each day's creation is good.

To show His love for man, God created him after He prepared everything for him. It is like a mother preparing for the delivery of a child. It is the instinctive love of the unborn child that drives a mother to prepare everything necessary before his/her arrival. So, as His children, He prepared everything for our livelihood. Not just for our livelihood, but also for us to marvel nature itself so that we can seek Him and grow in the knowledge and love of the maker of this beautiful world. That is why King David said, *"The heavens declare the glory of God and the firmament shows His handywork. Day unto day utters speech and night unto night shows knowledge."* /Psalm 19:1-2/

His love is also manifested in creating man on the sixth day, for He created man not just as His subject, but also as a king on earth. Marveling about this act of love, King David said, You *"have crowned Him with glory and honor, You made Him to have dominion over the works of Your hands. You have put all things under His foot."* /Psalm 8:5-6/.

A king makes an arrival after everything due in his honor is prepared beforehand. Regarding the reasons for creating man last of all creation, St. Gregory of Nyssa wrote the following:

It was not to be looked for that the ruler should appear before the subjects of his rule; but when his dominion was prepared, the next step was that the king should be manifested. When, then, the Maker of all had prepared beforehand, as it were, a royal lodging for the future king (and this was the land, and islands, and sea, and the heaven arching like a roof over them), and when all kinds of wealth had been stored in this palace (and by wealth I mean the whole creation, all that is in plants and trees, and all that has sense, and breath, and life; and — if we are to account materials also as wealth— all that for their beauty are reckoned precious in the eyes of men, as gold and silver, and the substances of your jewels which men delight in — having concealed, I say, abundance of all these also in the bosom of the earth as in a royal treasure-house), he thus manifests man in the world, to be the beholder of some of the wonders therein, and the lord of others; that by his enjoyment he might have knowledge of the Giver, and by the beauty and majesty of the things he saw might trace out that power of the Maker which is beyond speech and language. (CHURCH FATHERS: On the Making of Man, ST. Gregory of Nyssa, n.d.)

After creating man on the sixth day of creation, it is written that God ended His work, and rested on the seventh day from all His work. /Gen. 2:2/. St Ephrem the Syrian asks, *"From what toil did God rest?"* God does not labor and tire like man. St. Ephrem also notes that God created all creation by "a gesture" or by His word. What toil did He rest from then?

Regarding the seventh day, St. Ephrem says that the seventh day is given to man to *"depict by temporal rest... the mystery of the true rest, which will be given to the eternal people in the eternal world."4* So, we can see that even though man is the last creation, he is also the crown of creation[5] – for everything on earth was created for mankind, and even the seventh day, on which God did not create anything, was given as a symbol of the kingdom God has prepared for eternal inheritance.

IV. Creating man in His own image and likeness.

*"I will praise You,
For I am fearfully and wonderfully made."
Psalm 139:14*

Since the first day of creation, angels wondered about the likeness of their creator. The devil, the father of lies, tried to convince the hosts of angels that He was their creator. He managed to deceive some, but He was cast out of heaven with his angels: *"And there was war in heaven: Michael and his angels fought against the dragon ... And the great dragon was cast out, that old serpent, called the Devil, and Satan, who deceives the whole world: he was cast out into the earth, and his angels were cast out with him." /Rev. 12:7-9/.*

---

[4] Ephrem The Syrian on Genesis 2:2 - Catena Bible & Commentaries. (n.d.). Catena Bible & Commentaries.
[5] Dogmatic Theology, by Protopresbyter Michael Pomazansky, 1983

The creation of man was a joyful occasion for them, because they would get to see a creature in the image and likeness of their creator, for God, before creating man, said: *"Let us make man in Our image, according to Our likeness." /Gen. 1:26/*

Man was the creature through whom God would manifest Himself to all creation. The whole creation speaks of God. *"The heavens declare the glory of God, and the firmament show His handiwork." /Psalm 19:1/.* But man, unlike other creations, is the image of God – a creature of both the material and the spiritual elements – a rationale, articulate and an ever-living creature. A creation that is not only in the image of God, but also bearing the breath of God. *"And the Lod God formed man of the dust of the ground, and beathed into his nostrils the breath of life." /Gen. 2:7/.*

Man is created from four material elements: earth, water, fire, and wind (air). Each of these material elements symbolize four essential attributes of the Lord God:

a. Earth symbolizes His affluence.

Man is made from the earth, but not the fallen earth. The fallen earth was condemned because of the fall of Adam and Eve: *"cursed is the ground for your sake; in sorrow shall you eat of it all the days of your life; Thorns also and thistles shall it bring forth to you. /Gen. 3:17-18/*. Before the fall, Adam and Eve were to eat the fruit of the earth with thanksgiving and joy. But after turning away from God, they would labor and eat from it *"in sorrow."* So, it is not the fallen earth, but the virgin earth – which brought forth all kinds of herbs and plants without being toiled - we are referring to.

The earth is the foundation for all other creations on planet earth as we can see in these words of the Lord God: *"Let the earth bring forth..." /Gen. 1:11,24/* It brought forth all that we need for our livelihood. It had seemingly infinite resources it provides for us, but we know that its resources are limited. The Lord God also provides for us infinitely, but there is no lacking in His affluence. For every element that comes from the earth, the earth lacks that amount of element that comes out of it. But because of its abundant resources, the little that it lacks is not noticeable. But we say that there is no lacking in God's affluence, because, unlike the earth, the treasure of His affluence does never diminish because of what He gives. It is of this unique attribute of God's affluence that St. Paul speaks of when He said, *"... the same Lord over all is rich unto all that call upon Him." /Rom. 10/*.

b. Water symbolizes His mercifulness.

Water cleanses that which is dirty. God, in His abundant mercy, cleanses us from our sins. It is because of His abundant mercy that we receive the grace of childhood, lost after the Fall, through baptism with water. Water also quenches or satisfies our thirst. There is nothing that can satisfy the human soul more so than the love and mercy of God. In what is known as the sermon on the mount, the Lord Jesus Christ said, *"Blessed are they who do hunger and thirst after righteousness: for they shall be filled."* /Matt. 5:6/. Water may quench our thirst for a time, but the satisfaction from *"thirst for righteousness"* is never vanquished.

Water can also be powerful to move large rocks in its way. The love and mercy of God also softens and moves the hardest of hearts. The Lord God said, *"A new heart also will I give you, and a new spirit will I put within you: and I will take away the stony heart out of your flesh..."* /Ez. 36:26/. It is this love that softened the heart of the criminal on the right of the crucified Christ, to ask for forgiveness.

c. Wind symbolizes God's judgment.

Wind separates seed from chaff. God also separates the righteous and sinners in his perfect judgment: *"He shall separate one from another as shepherd divides his sheep from his goats. /Matt. 25:32/.* We do not know where wind comes from, but we only hear of its sound: *"The wind blows where it wishes, and you hear the sound thereof, but can't tell where it comes from and where it goes." /John 3:8/.* Likewise, God is unsearchable, and His essence is unknown. We know Him only by His works through which He reveals Himself to us. We also share in this mystical nature of God because we ourselves receive the invisible grace of childhood through the visible rites of Baptism with water.

d. Fire symbolizes God's greatness and might.

Speaking of the greatness and might of God's glory, St. Paul wrote, *"God is a consuming fire." /Heb. 12:29/* Fire destroys everything in its path unless restrained or contained by water or a physical barrier. The wrath of God is also a consuming fire unless restrained by His own infinite love and mercifulness.

We can see the love of God for us through these material elements of our body which symbolize essential attributes of God, and through the spiritual elements by which we are granted the image the likeness of the Creator.

The phrase *"in our image and likeness"* is also an indication of our likeness to the second person of the Holy Trinity, the Son of God who would be incarnate four our salvation. St. Basil, speaking of this said: *"... does not the second Person show Himself in a mystical way, without yet manifesting Himself until the great day?"*[6]

The Lord God, who has dominion over all creation, gave man dominion over everything on earth. The words "in the image and likeness" of God is also a reference to this dominion over all creation on earth. St. Ephrem wrote, *"It is the dominion that Adam received over the earth and over all that is in it that constitutes the likeness of God who has dominion over the heavenly things and the earthly things."*[7]

V.   God's deliberation before creating man.

"Let us make man in our image, after our likeness." /Gen. 1:25/

One of the unique aspects of the creation of man is the deliberation we see before his making. We do not see anything like it in the creation of any of the other creations. But we see a clear deliberation in the words of God when He says, *"let us create man in our image after our own likeness."* These words show not just God's intent and reason in creating man, but also in creating everything on earth before man, because we

---

[6] Basil the Great on Genesis 1:26 - Catena Bible & Commentaries. (n.d.). Catena Bible & Commentaries.

[7] Ephrem The Syrian on Genesis 1:26 - Catena Bible & Commentaries. (n.d.). Catena Bible & Commentaries.

also see words of deliberation and intent for man's relationship with nature: *"... and let them have dominion over the fish of the sea, and over the fowl of the air, and over the cattle, and over all the earth, and over every creeping thing that creeps upon the earth." /Gen. 1:25/* From these words, we understand that even though man was created last, everything created before man was created for him. God's love for man even before man was created is manifested in these words of deliberation.

The Lord God did not bring man into existence by simply saying *"Let there be man"* as He had done in bringing forth other creations on earth. Man was unique and the Lord wanted to express His love and desire to create man in His own image and likeness through these words of deliberation. St. Gregory of Nyssa wrote, *"God deliberated about the best way to bring to life a creation worthy of honor." (CHURCH FATHERS: On the Making of Man (ST. Gregory of Nyssa), n.d.)*

God, of course was not talking to anyone one when He said *"Let us..."* It is a self-deliberation, on the one hand so that angels can hear His voice and anticipate this precious being that would be created in the image of God. On the other hand, it is to show us that we are created in the image of each person of the Trinity. And affirming that we are created only in the image of God, and not in the image of any other beings besides God, it is written, *"So God created man in his own image, in the image of God created*

He him; male and female created He them." /Gen. 1:27/

VI. Making Eve from Adam's ribs

"It is not good that man should be alone... And the Lord God caused a deep sleep to fall on Adam, and he slept/ and He took one of his ribs and closed up the flesh in its place. Then the rib which the Lord God had taken from man, He made it into a woman..." /Gen. 2:18 – 22/

About the creation of man, it is written that He created them male and female. /Gen. 1:27/. That is because Eve was inside Adam and would be formed from his ribs. The words, *"It is not good that man should be alone...,"* are words of affection and care. It shows that God did not bring forth creation for His satisfaction – but rather for the benefit of His most precious creation – mankind. That is why He prepared everything good for mankind, before creating him. And these words show His continued care.

The way He gave Adam a companion is a testament to His continued love and care. He did not create man like other animals – separately as male and female. He created Adam and, in his bosom, Eve. Like Adam, He formed Eve with His own hands – but not from the dust of the ground. He formed Eve from the right ribs of Adam. The

Lord God created them in this manner so that His love for them would naturally be reflected between Adam and Eve. And this was reflected immediately in the words of Adam. When He woke up from his sleep and saw Eve, he said: *"This is now bone of my bones and flesh of my flesh."* Gen. 2:23

It also is not without reason God made Eve from Adam's ribs. It is to show that Eve is an equal to Adam, comparable to Him – for she is made not from bones below the ribs, and not above either – but from the middle of his body – his ribs. This of course is important not just for a harmonic relationship, but for the satisfaction of both Adam and Eve. Adam was not alone in the Garden of Eden, but he was lonely, because there was none equal and comparable to Him. That is why He expressed His joy in a unique manner when He saw eve in the words we have seen above. A companion not comparable to him would not be sufficient to get rid of his loneliness. That is why it is written, *"...for Adam there was not found a helper suitable for him."* /Gen. 2:20/. Therefore, the Lord God said, *"I will make him a helper suitable for him."* /Gen. 2:18/.

One may be inclined to think that Eve is an afterthought in creation – that she was only created after God noticed Adam's loneliness. But that is not the case. It is exactly to show us His affection, His love, and His thoughtfulness for all our needs that it so happened in this manner. Such degree of order in the story of creation is to teach us that the Lord God is a God of reason, who did not create arbitrarily simply because of His might, but according to reason, and out of His love for creation – especially for the one He created in His own image.

VII. The Tree of Knowledge

Why did God create the tree of knowledge of good and bad? This is a question many, including faithful Christians, ask. The general notion for this is that if He had not created it, man would not sin. Is it created to simply tempt Adam? Would Adam not have sinned if He were not given such commandment? Is it because of this tree that Adam sinned? ... We can ask many questions about this forbidden fruit. Contemplating on the reason for the Tree of knowledge though, we come to understand of God's love reflected through it, in many ways.

i. A symbol of Freedom

The Tree of knowledge is a symbol of freedom – a means by which man can freely choose whether to worship and love God or not. But with freedom of course comes consequences for one's choice. The Lord God told Adam and

Eve of the consequence of eating from this fruit. *"Of every tree of the garden you may freely eat, but of the tree of knowledge of good and evil, you shall not it, for in the day you eat of it, you shall surely die."* **Gen. 2:16-17**

One may ask, why offer this opportunity – the freedom to choose? Why is freedom not accorded to any other creation, but given to man? The answer is because we are created in the image of God – having the free will to choose our destiny. God is a rational and free being. Having intended and expressing His intention to create man in His own image and likeness, it is only fitting to give man the grace of free choice. Therefore, it is essential that there is a visible element through which man can exercise this freedom.

God gave Adam and Eve dominion over every living creature on earth: *"Let them have dominion over the fish of the sea, over the birds of the air, and over the cattle, over all the earth and over every creeping thing that creeps on the earth." /Gen. 1:26/.* None of these creatures had the freedom to choose whether to be subjects of man, because none was created in the image of God. But man was not to be God's subject in the same manner as all other creation on earth. This is one of the distinguishing characteristics of man – a rational being with freedom to choose. It would be contrary to God's nature therefore to say *"Let us create man in Our own image"* but deprive him of this attribute of His essence - the freedom to choose. Therefore, God made the Tree of Knowledge as a means for man to freely choose to be under God's dominion, to freely choose to be subject to Him who made every living creature on earth his subjects. St. Gregory the theologian said, God gave Adam & Eve *"a law as a material for his free will to act on."*[8]

ii. An object to value God's benevolence

"... I have learned both to be full and to be hungry, both to abound and to suffer need." **Ph. 4:12**

A person who has everything at his disposal has less or no appreciation than another who has experienced lacking. St. Paul said, *"I have learned both to be full and to be hungry, both to abound and to suffer need." /Philip. 4:12/*. He spoke these words because there is much to benefit from suffering need as from having abound. He thanked the Philippians for sharing in his distress. This shows that a

---

[8] Azzi, E. (2018, December 13). Why did God plant the Tree of Knowledge of Good and Evil? Coptic Orthodox Answers. https://copticorthodoxanswers.org/general/why-did-god-plant-the-tree-of-knowledge-of-good-and-evil/

stronger bond is formed in sharing in someone's needs or lacking. It was so that Adam & Eve could have a stronger bond through love with God, that they had to experience lacking, so that in what they had abundantly, they can better understand the love of God. After expressing his gratitude to those who sent him gifts, St. Paul ended his gratitude with these words: *"Now to our God and Father be glory forever and ever. Amen."* /Ph. 4:20/

Adam and Eve would never experience lacking in the garden of Eden without the forbidden fruit. They would have lacked the perspective to value the benevolence of God, without the presence of something that they could not touch. The tree of knowledge was to serve that purpose. Realizing that God forbid them from eating the fruit of one from among countless in the Garden of Eden. Now they had one thing they could not touch, but too many to count to appreciate the benevolence of God and say, *"to our benevolent God be glory."*

iii.   An object of fairness

"You will judge the people with fairness."
Psalm 67:4

One of the most consistent opinions we hear about the tree of knowledge is that it just seems like a trap, and that if this Tree of Knowledge were not there, man would never have fallen from grace. But if we go back to the first day of creation, there was no such 'trap' that caused the fall of Satan. Sin therefore did not enter the world by any one action due to an external object of desire, but by Satan's prideful state of mind and declaration of himself among the angels as their creator.

Was it also possible for Adam and Eve to sin in the absence of the Tree of Knowledge? If an angel could sin just by having sinful thought, man is also certainly capable of it. In fact, the fall of Adam and Eve started with a sinful thought – a desire to be like God. This desire was manifested in the rebellious act of Adam & Eve against the commandment of God in eating the forbidden fruit.

It might seem unfair if man would be punished only for his sinful desire, because no one knows the inner desire of a man, except God. But this inner desire was manifest in the act of eating from the forbidden fruit – the tree of knowledge. This tree was no more beautiful or attractive than other trees in the garden of Eden. But, when Eve saw it with a sinful desire because of the serpent's deceptive words, she *"saw that the tree was good for food, and that it was pleasant to the eyes, and a tree to be desired to make one wise..." /Gen. 3:6/.*

As perfectly loving and just as God is, He chose to place the tree of knowledge in the garden of Eden as an object of fairness. That is why, after the transgression, the Lord God came to Adam and asked, *"Have you eaten from the tree of which I commanded you that you should not eat?"*

Commenting on this forbidden tree as a symbol of fairness in God's justice, St. Ephrem said, *"God had given to Adam everything inside and outside Paradise through Grace, requiring nothing in return, either for his creation, or for the glory in which He had clothed him,* **nevertheless out of Justice He held back one tree from him** *to whom He had given, in Grace, everything in Paradise and on earth, in the air and in the seas."*[9]

iv. An object of obedience & love

There is no limit to God's grace. In addition to all that He had done for man in creation, He would grant him greater grace. But for that to happen, there had to be a harmony of love between God and man. This harmony could

---

[9] Ephrem The Syrian on Genesis 3:6 - Catena Bible & Commentaries. (n.d.). Catena Bible & Commentaries.

exist only when man can grow in the love of God. It is through a growing love that man can learn more about God and share in His divine attribute of love. But love is real only when it can be expressed in some manner. The tree of knowledge was this object of obedience and love through which man can express and grow in his love for God through obedience. That is why our Lord and Savior Jesus Christ said, *"If you love me, keep my commandments."*

Through obedience, not only would they grow in their knowledge and grace of God, but Adam and Eve would also grow to love each other more and more – for that is the foundation of harmony in marriage. God's love for us is to be reflected in a matrimonial relationship too. That is why St. Paul said, *"Husbands, love your wives, just as Christ also loved the church."* **Eph. 5:25.**

Through obedience, Adam and Eve were going to be rewarded with more grace so that they would continue to experience the love of God and grow in their knowledge of love – not just in receiving one, but also in giving one by continuing their obedience to the God of infinite grace. There is nothing they would add to the glory of God by learning to give love. But their own joy would be greater. The joy of giving is something that can only be experienced through such act of love. It is written that God is love, because of His immeasurable act of love in giving. In the act of giving love through obedience, Adam and Eve would abide in the love of God. That is why the forbidden fruit is considered an object of love.

Chapter 3

God's love after the fall

"Where are you?" Gen. 3:9

God did not just tell Adam not to eat from the Tree of Knowledge, but also the consequence of eating from it. He did this so that Adam and Eve could exercise temperance – knowing that there is an undesirable consequence for the wrong choices in life. It was a commandment of love. It is what loving parents would do. When the child is not yet able to discern the dangers of a certain action, the parents would somehow like to warn the child or make the child aware of the dangerous consequence of his/her action. Adam and Eve were yet children and did not have the full grasp of the love of God. If they did, that alone would have been enough for them to exercise temperance. St Ephrem said, to give them another element of temperance *"God withheld from him a single tree, hedging it around with death, so that even if Adam were to fail to keep the law out of love for the Lawgiver, at least the fear of death that surrounded the tree would make him afraid of overstepping the law."*[10]

---

[10] Ephrem The Syrian on Genesis 2:17 - Catena Bible & Commentaries. (n.d.). Catena Bible & Commentaries; *Hymns on*

Instead of heading to the commandment of God who had given them dominion over all creation on earth, they hearkened to the deceptive words of the serpent – who gave them nothing. Neither the love of God, nor the fear of death caused them to exercise temperance and question the serpent. They ate from the forbidden fruit and brought the judgement of death upon themselves. Speaking of this, St. Athanasius wrote, *""Men had turned from the contemplation of God above, and were looking for Him in the opposite direction, down among created things and things of sense."*[11]

As soon as they ate of this forbidden fruit, they lost the grace of God and learned that they were naked. They were covered by the grace of God, but now they had to sew fig leaves to cover their nakedness. Fear came upon them for the first time in the Garden, and they tried to hide from God: When the Lord came into the garden and asked Adam, *'Where are you?" Adam replied, "I heard your voice in the garden, and I was afraid, because I was naked; and I hid myself." /Gen. 3:9/*. Man, that was made king of all creation on earth, now sought to hide among his subjects.

Turning their thought from the creator to a deceptive creature led them to transgression, and instead of turning back to God, they looked further away from

---

Paradise (Popular Patristics Series) | Logos Bible Software, https://www.logos.com/product/161354/hymns-on-paradise.
[11] (n.d.). On the Incarnation. Christian Classics Ethereal Library.

Him in their hiding. But He did not want to leave them on their path of destruction. The loving and merciful God, did not leave them to perish, but He came to them and called them with love: *"Where are you?" /Gen. 3:9/.* They turned themselves away from Him, but His eyes were always on them. They did not repent and seek Him, but He came seeking to save them from eternal corruption. These words of the Lord speak to His love for those who rejected Him: *"I am sought of them that asked not for me; I am found of them that sought me not" /Is. 65:1/.*

No one can hide from the presence of God: *"Where can I go from Your Spirit? Or where can I flee from your presence?" /Psalm 139:7/.* God asked Adam where he was, so that Adam would acknowledge his transgression and come forth. This was the first time Adam experienced fear in the Garden. But God wanted him to come forth from his hiding. That is why he asked, *"Where are you?"* Through the ears that hearkened to words of deception poured in words of love and affection. How marvelous, soft, and kind the words of God must have been, when He called on Adam, saying *"Where are you?"*

The Lord God could have simply come to Adam and Eve and pass on the judgement of death that He had warned them of. But instead, He spoke words of affection, words of one searching for something precious, a voice of love, calling him to come out from his hiding – from a path of destruction. God did not wait for them to come clean on their own from their hiding: *"Where are you?"* The Lord Jesus Christ, speaking about His loving desire to restore Adam to his former place, spoke these words in the gospel: *"If a man has a hundred sheep, and one of them be gone astray, does he not leave the ninety and nine, and go into the mountains, and seek that which is gone astray? And if so be that he finds it, verily I say unto you, he rejoices more for that sheep, than for the ninety and nine which went not astray. /Matt. 18:12-13/*

Adam replied to the Lord's call saying that He was naked and therefore hid himself. But the Lord God continued, again with a soft and loving tone, and asked Adam: *"who told you that you were naked? Have you eaten from the tree of which I commanded you that you should not eat?" /Gen 3:11/.* He wanted to give Adam an opportunity to acknowledge his sins, for this was the first and most important step to a path for repentance. But because of his grave fear from his transgression, Adam could not feel the love of God in the words of His affectionate calling. Instead, he presented an excuse for his fault: *"The woman whom You gave to be with me, she gave me of the tree, and I ate." /Gen. 3:13/.* By saying *the woman whom You gave to be with me..."* Adam was not just blaming Eve, but also implicating God himself. But God went to Eve, and asked why she did this. She also put the blame on the serpent.

At this time, the Lord God turned to the serpent admonishing it for what it had done. As king and queen of everything on earth, they had the opportunity to admonish the serpent and thereby admonish the devil disguised in it. What they had failed to do, the Lord God did – He admonished it– and then declared to this old serpent – that his deception was not going to cause a lasting demise of mankind saying: *"I will put enmity between you and the woman, and between your seed and her Seed. He shall bruise your head, and you shall bruise His heel." /Gen. 3:15/.* The devil's plan was to foil God's plan for His most esteemed creation – man. But the fall was not going to cause a lasting demise of man and foil God's plan. That is what the Lord God revealed in His words to the serpent. God in fact had a plan to restore man to his former state – because God is love and therefore it is not characteristic of His essence to let man perish.

When the Lord came to Adam and Eve, he asked them what they had done. Even though He knew what they did, before pronouncing judgement, He gave them a chance to answer for their transgressions. Speaking of this extraordinary gesture, St. John Chrysostom said, *"See the Lord's loving kindness and the surpassing degree of his longsuffering. I mean, though being in a position to begrudge such great sinners the right of reply and rather than to consign them at once to the punishment he had determined in anticipation of their transgression, He shows patience and withholds action. He asks a question, receives a reply, and questions them further as if inviting them to excuse themselves so that he might seize the opportunity to display his characteristic love in regard to the sinners, even despite their fall."*[12]

When the Lord God came to Adam and Eve, he asked them what they had done, but when He turned to the serpent, He did not ask. Instead, He immediately spoke of judgment saying, *"Because you have done this, you are cursed above all cattle, and above every beast of the field; upon your belly shall you go, and dust shall you eat all the days of your life." /Gen. 3:14/* . Then before turning to Adam and Eve and pronouncing judgment against them, He first spoke words of defeat against the devil that was disguised in the serpent – which were words of the hope of salvation for Adam and Eve: *"And I will put enmity between you and the woman, and between your seed and her seed; he shall bruise your head, and you shall bruise his heel." /Gen. 3:15/*. The Lord did this to let them know that they are destined for redemption.

God came to Adam and Eve the same day they transgressed His commandment. Even though Adam and Eve chose to try and hide from Him, He came to them for He is a loving father. The Lord Jesus Christ

---

[12] G. (n.d.). Genesis 3 - Catena Bible & Commentaries. Catena Bible & Commentaries. https://catenabible.com/gn/3

spoke about this fatherly love in the parable of "The Prodigal Son." */Luke 15/*. After the son left his father's house with his portion, he wasted it riotously after going to a faraway country. But when he had no one to help him, after he wasted all his money, he repented in his heart and returned to his father's house. And *"when he was yet a great way off, his father saw him, and had compassion, and ran, and fell on his neck, and kissed him." /Luke 15:20/*

The father was the first to have a glimpse of his son, while he was still far off, because he had always been waiting for his son to return. His searching eyes were wandering as far as he could see, hoping that his son would come back. And when he saw him, the first emotion he felt was compassion out of love. Before the son uttered any words of penitence, he fell on his neck and kissed him. He made a feast, saying, *"For this my son was dead, and is alive again; he was lost, and is found." /Luke 15:24/*. This parable is about the Lord God, who loves us without conditions. He never forgets us, no matter how far off we may have distanced ourselves from him because of sin. And it is such unconditional love that is manifested in the affectionate words of the Lord God for Adam after the fall: *"Where are you?"*

God's plan for the salvation of mankind was based on His unconditional love for His most precious creation. That is why, even though Adam and Eve tried to find blame for their transgression, He spoke to the serpent, words of His plan to foil its deception and to save Adam and Eve.

What is it that the Lord God revealed in these words? It is His incarnation for our salvation. "The woman" is the Virgin Mary. "Her Seed" is the incarnate Son of God – our Lord and savior Jesus Christ. Saying *"He shall bruise your head..."* He revealed that He would defeat the devil and destroy his work of deception. The Lord God spoke these words of hope before He pronounced judgement for their transgression – so that they would know that they are not eternally condemned; therefore, they would live with the hope of being saved.

If God in His abundant love goes to those who try to hide from His presence, how much more does He lovingly receive those who repent and come to Him seeking His mercy? As the father who received the prodigal son, He would receive us with joy. That is why the Lord Jesus Christ said, *"... joy shall be in heaven over one sinner that repents, more than over ninety and nine just persons, who need no repentance." /Luke 15:7/*. This is a kind of love that is hard to imagine. What manner of love is this that causes more joy in heaven for the repentance of a sinner than those who are righteous? What manner of love is this that drives one to go after his transgressor, not to take vengeance seeking retribution, but seeking to forgive, and to pay for the debt of the transgressor?

Chapter 4

God's love after the promise of salvation

"And the Lord was sorry that He had made man on the earth, and He was grieved in His heart." Gen. 6:6

After the fall, Adam and Eve were cast out of paradise. Even though God promised to save them, their children continued to rebel against God. Moses expressed how much mankind grieved the Lord God, saying, *"And the Lord was sorry that He had made man on the earth, and He was grieved in His heart." /Gen. 6:6/*. What loving mother or father would not be grieved if his or her child were to choose a self-destructive path? "The grief" due to man's descent into corruption comes from God's love for his people. It is only to express how much God was grieved that Moses wrote that the Lord was sorry that He had made man. If He really regretted it, He could have simply ended the existence of mankind.

From the first sons of Adam and Eve, Abel & Cain, until the appointed time of the Lord Jesus Christ's advent, mankind had been rebelling against God.

But God's promise of salvation did not depend on the righteousness of mankind. The Lord Jesus Christ, speaking to a chief of the Pharisees, Nicodemus, said *"For God so loved the world, that he gave his only begotten Son" /John 3:16/*. So loved – means not with any precondition, not in response to any external action, but that He simply loved us. This is a love that cannot be defined in words but could only be manifest in His redeeming sacrifice. Even though man did not deserve the fulfillment of this promise, the Lord God continued to re-affirm this covenant of love – the promise of salvation – throughout generations. Even though many continued to rebel against Him, there were few righteous with whom the Lord God made a covenant.

I. The Covenant of Noah

Because of the sins of the children of God on earth, Moses wrote, *"And the LORD was sorry that He had made man on the earth, and it grieved him to his heart." /Gen. 6:6/*. During the time of Noah, there was no one righteous found on earth except him. Because of this, the Lord said, *"I will destroy man whom I have created from the face of the earth." /Gen. 6:7/*. But the Lord God commanded Noah, who had found grace in the sight Lord, to build an Ark to save himself and his family. After the great flood, everyone outside of the Ark perished. But Noah and his family came out and worshipped the Lord God who protected them from the flood. It is because of the grave sins of mankind that Moses wrote, *"And the LORD was sorry that he had made man on the earth, and it grieved him to his heart."*

This is written to show how much man has grieved the Lord God. But God, of course, does not regret what He does as man does, for He is always right in His might, righteous in His judgement and merciful in His wrath. That is why, after Noah and his family came of out the Ark, the Lord promised not to destroy the earth again because of man. He made a covenant with Noah and all creation saying, *"This is the token of the covenant which I make between me and you and every living creature that is with you, for perpetual generations: I do set my bow in the cloud, and it shall be for a token of a covenant between me and the earth. And it shall come to pass, when I bring a cloud over the earth, that the bow shall be seen in the cloud: And I will remember my covenant, which is between me and you and every living creature of all flesh; and the waters shall no more become a flood to destroy all flesh. And the bow shall be in the cloud; and I will look upon it, that I may remember the everlasting covenant between God and every living creature of all flesh that is upon the earth."* /Gen. 9:12-16/

Does God really need a reminder for His covenant, that He said, *"... the bow shall be seen in the cloud, and I will remember"?* Certainly not. He, who called us to be holy as He himself is holy said this only to give us a sign to remember His love and His covenant – which He makes with us out of His abundant love. That is why He said: *"Beware that you do not forget the Lord your God, in not keeping His commandments." /Deut. 8:11/. "The covenant I have made with you, you shall not forget." /2 Kings 17:38/.*

His love is manifested in saving humanity because of the righteousness of one man, instead of utter destruction because of the sins of many. Noah found favor before God because of His righteousness – and because of him, God preserved humanity and made a covenant with Noah: *"I will never again curse the earth because of man's works, although the mind of a man is diligently involved with evil things from his youth; nor will I again destroy every living thing as I have done..." /Gen. 8:21-22/.* And the Lord God blessed Noah and his sons with the same blessing that He blessed Adam and Eve after creation: *"Increase and multiply, and fill the earth, and have dominion over it..." /Gen. 9:1).* This manifests that God's love for mankind does not wane out.

II. The Covenant of Melchizedek

Melchizedek is known as the King of Salem, whose priesthood is a symbol of Christ. Speaking of this, king David and St. Paul said, *"You are a priest after the order of Melchizedek."* /Psalm110:4; Heb. 5:10/. Melchizedek's priesthood was superior to the priesthood of the Levites, because:

- He was ordained before the Levitical priesthood and was greater than Abraham – for Abraham received blessing from him. /Gen. 14/
- His priesthood is never ending and a symbol to the eternal priesthood of our Lord and Savior Jesus Christ.
- Received a tithe from the Levites through Abraham: *"... but he whose genealogy is not derived from them received tithes from Abraham and blessed him who had the promises... Even Levi, who receives tithes, paid tithes through Abraham, so to speak, for he was still in the loins of his father when Melchizedek met him."* /Heb. 7:5-10/
- He is not ordained in the manner of the Levitical priesthood with a sacrifice and by anointing with oil, but the Lord God chose him and ordained him with a holy order symbolic of the Priesthood of our Lord and

savior Jesus Christ. The Lord Jesus Christ is the high priest who offered Himself as the ultimate sacrifice of our salvation.

Therefore, God's covenant of our salvation was re-affirmed in the priesthood of Melchizedek.

III. The Covenant of Abraham

Abraham left his father's house and the country of his relatives when he was 75 years old, heading to God's commandment: *"Get out of your country, from your kindred and from your father's house to a land I will show you. I will make you a great nation. I will bless you and make your name great…"* /Gen. 12: 1-2/. God also made a covenant with Abraham saying, *"I will establish My covenant between Me and you, and will multiply you exceedingly… You shall be a father of many nations. /Gen. 17:2 – 4/* The Lord God also revealed to him the Covenant of His love and mercy for our salvation. The Lord Jesus Christ spoke of this saying, *"Your father Abraham rejoiced to see My day, and he saw it and was glad."* /John 8:56/. It is when Abraham offered his son Isaac that he saw 'the Lord's Day' and rejoiced.

God tested Abraham and said, *"Take now your beloved Son, Isaac, whom you love and go to the land of Moriah and offer him there as a whole burnt offering…"* /Gen. 22:1/. This is the first time we see the word "love" in the Bible. The Lord God did not just ask him to offer Isaac, but *"your beloved Son, Isaac, whom you love."* It was so that Abrahm, through his absolute faith in the promise He received from God, would foresee God's own faithfulness to fulfil His promise of salvation which He first made right after the fall of Adam & Eve.

Abraham did not hesitate to sacrifice His son Isaac. Isaac was the son he had at an old age. He was the son God promised, and this promise was fulfilled after both Abraham and Sarah were past the age childbearing. The Lord God also promised to multiply Abraham's seed through Isaac like the stars in heaven and the sands on earth. But Abraham did not hesitate to sacrifice Isaac, believing that *"God was able to raise him up, even from the dead." /Heb 11:19/*.

The Lord God also gave *"His only begotten Son, that whoever believes in Him should not perish but have everlasting life." /John 3:16/*. Through this extraordinary show of faith, Abraham saw the promise of eternal salvation. That is why St. Paul wrote, *"By faith Abraham obeyed when he was called to go out to the place which he would receive as an inheritance... for he waited for the city which has **foundations, whose builder and maker is God.*** */Heb. 11:8-10/*

The city, the builder and maker of which is God, is the eternal inheritance, God's kingdom. Hoping for this eternal inheritance, Abraham *"dwelt in the land of promise." /Heb 11:9/*.

IV.   The Covenant of Moses

The Lord God continued to reveal His promise of salvation to Moses, while the Israelites were under bondage, in Egypt. He was born about four hundred years after the Israelites were exiled to Egypt due to famine. Because of the growing number of the Israelites, the Egyptians felt threatened, and the Pharaoh subjected them to extreme labor under the bondage of slavery. Moses was born during this time, and at a time when there was a decree to kill all male child born of an Israelite.

His mother kept him for a while after giving birth, but when she could no longer hide him, she put him in a basket and left him in a river. The Pharoah's daughter found Moses in the river and took him as her son, making him an eventual heir to the Pharaoh. After Moses grew up, he was forced to flee from the Pharaoh's house because he killed an Egyptian to protect an Israelite.

After Moses was exiled from the house of the Pharoah to the land of the Midian, he noticed a burning bush on the "mountain of God," while keeping the flock of his father-in-law, Jethro. In this extraordinary scene, Moses saw *"the woman" and "her seed"* /Gen. 3:15/. This was a symbolic scene of the incarnation of God the Son, in the womb of the Virgin Mary – and as the burning bush was not consumed by the fire, the Virgin May was not consumed by Divine Fire.

God sent Moses to deliver Israel from Pharaoh. Moses himself was a prefigure to the eternal deliverer, the incarnate Son of God, the Lord Jesus Christ, who would deliver His people from the bondage of sin. And while leading the Israelites out of Egypt, Moses received "the tables of the Covenant." /Deut. 9:9/. The stone tablets are symbols of the Virgin Mary and the words on them, the eternal Word of God – our Lord and Savior Jesus Christ.

Speaking about how, with much zeal and devotion, Moses had faith in what was revealed to him, St. Paul wrote: *"By faith Moses, when he was come to years, refused to be called the son of the Pharaoh's daughter; choosing rather to suffer affliction with the people of God, than to enjoy the pleasures of sin for a season. Esteeming the reproach of Christ greater riches than the treasures of Egypt."* /Heb. 11:24-26/.

It is interesting that Moses gives greater value to the reproach of the Lord Jesus Christ than the treasures of Egypt. He did so because he saw the love of God even in His reproach. What Adam and Eve failed to see in God's divine benevolence, Moses saw in God's reproach. What is the reproach of Christ? It is the suffering that Moses had to endure, for in such a reproach, *"he looked for the recompense of the reward"*/Heb. 11:26/ from the Lord Jesus Christ –

whom He saw in the covenant the Lord made with the righteous fathers.

Moses is also a prefigure of the Lord Jesus Christ in many ways. As He forsook the riches of Egypt and chose to suffer with His people, the Son of God humbled himself to partake of our nature, and He dwelt among us, suffered, and died for us. Egypt, the land where the Israelites lived for hundreds of years in bondage, is a symbol of the earth, in which Adam was exiled and lived under the bondage of sin. The promise land, which the Lord God gave to the Israelites is a symbol of God's eternal kingdom, which He prepared for us from the foundation of the world. Passing through the Red Sea is a symbol of baptism, by which we are adopted as the children of God and became heirs to God's Kingdom. In general, the deliverance of the Israelites from the bondage of Egypt is a symbol of humanity's deliverance by our Lord and Savior Jesus Christ from the bondage of sin, for an eternal salvation.

V. The Covenant of David

The Lord's promise of salvation is especially reaffirmed in what He revealed to his servant David. That is why we see so much prophecy not just about the incarnation of the Son of God, but about His virgin birth, His baptism, His ministry, His miracles, His suffering, His crucifixion, His death, His resurrection, and His ascension.

The Lord promised David, *"I will set upon your throne the fruit of your body." /Ps. 132:11/* He said this for the time about David's son, Solomon. But it was a prophecy about the incarnation of God the Son. This becomes clear in the words that follow this promise: *"For the Lord has chosen Zion. He has desired her for His dwelling place." /Ps. 132:13/* Zion, the dwelling place the Lord God desired, is the Virgin Mary, from whom He partook of our nature and became man for our salvation.

Knowing that the covenant of salvation the Lord promised first to Adam and Eve would be fulfilled from the fruit of his body, St. Ephrem the Syrian wrote, " *(King David) wished to seek out and to prepare a dwelling place for God, the Word of the Father… and he cried out in the Holy Spirit: "behold we heard of it in Ephratah, the dwelling place of the God of Jacob, which is Bethlehem, in which Emmanuel has chosen to be born in the flesh for our salvation"* /Thursday's Praise of Mary; Psalm 132:6/

Speaking of God's unconditional love and the covenant He made with Adam and which He affirmed to him, king David said, *"The Lord has sworn in truth to David and He shall not repent." /Ps. 132:11/* The Lord God's promise of salvation and its fulfillment did not depend on anything external to Him, but only on His unconditional and unyielding love for man. That is why, it is said, *"He shall not repent.*" And that is why He reaffirmed the promise He gave Adam, as a covenant with David, saying, *"I will put upon your throne the fruit of your body."*

Chapter 5

God's love in the fulfillment of His promise

"In this was manifested the love of God toward us, because God sent his only begotten Son into the world, that we might live through him."
1 John 4:9

God's unconditional love for mankind was also manifested in the fulfillment of His promise of Salvation – His incarnation. As we have already seen, the covenant He made with the righteous fathers about His coming into the world for our salvation was not tied to anything we had to do. *"In this was manifested the love of God toward us because God sent his only begotten Son into the world, that we might live through him. In this is love, not that we loved God, but that He loved us, and sent His Son to be the propitiation for our sins. /1 John 4:9-10/.* If His promise of salvation were conditional on anything man would have to do, His incarnation would never have been a reality – because mankind would not have lived up to it. True love has no conditions tied to it. That is why St. Paul said, *"love never fails." /1 Cor. 13:8/*

Even though there were many righteous fathers in the old covenant, most people lived a life of sin and rebellion against the Lord God. Murder, hatred, idolatry, blasphemy, revelry, sexual immorality... were becoming increasingly the norm of the generation after the Fall. But the loving God did not keep account of the sinful deeds of mankind throughout many generations regarding fulfilling His promise. St. Paul said that love *"keeps no record of evil."* /*1. Cor. 13:5*/. Instead of keeping record of man's evil deeds from the killing of Abel until His coming, the Lord God kept reminding the Israelites of His promise through the prophets. But, as the Lord Jesus Christ spoke of what they did in a parable in the gospel of *Luke 20*, they killed the prophets. Yet, the Father sent His only begotten Son, knowing that they would do the same to Him.

At a time when it seemed like the evil of mankind could not get any worse and the descent into corruption continued, the Son of God came, according to the time appointed of His promise. St. Paul wrote, *"But when the fullness of the time came, God sent forth His Son, made of a woman, made under the law"* /*Gal. 4:4*/. This is truly a testament to the unconditional love in God's work of redemption. Man was created in a perfect world, but the Lord Jesus Christ was born in a corrupt world, to redeem man who brought corruption into the world. Man turned away from God and lost the grace of childhood, but the Son of God came in the direction man was looking to redeem him and adopt him as a child again. About this, St. Athanasius, in his writing "On the Incarnation" wrote, *"Men had turned from the contemplation of God above, and were looking for Him in the opposite direction, down among created things and things of sense. The Savior of us all, the Word of God, in His great love took to Himself a body and moved as Man among men, meeting their senses."* [13]

The Lord God showed His love to Adam & Eve in creation, and in His benevolence. He created great earthly and celestial wonders so that man could see God in the work of His grand and marvelous creation. But man failed to see His creator. So, the Son of God came in humility, *"taking the form of a bondservant, and coming in the likeness of men. And being found in appearance as a man, He humbled Himself..."* /Phil. 2:6-8/

In His birth, He humbled Himself. The King of the universe did not come to be born among the rich and the powerful, but from the most humble and holiest of all creations – the Virgin Mary. He was not born in a palace or the best of places, but in a manger among domestic animals. He did not magically or miraculously appear as a young man, but was conceived in the virgin's womb, born an infant, and grew up slowly according to the law of human nature.

---

[13] *St. Athanasius: On the Incarnation of the Word - Christian Classics ...*, https://ccel.org/ccel/athanasius/incarnation/incarnation.iv.html.

When the time was at hand, He did not send an army or delegations to announce His coming as kings do but sent forth John the Baptist – who grew up in the wilderness. After His birth, He did not send His angels to kings and queens to announce His advent, but He sent them to shepherds who were keeping their sheep in the middle of the night. He did all these so that, man who failed to see His creator in the grandeur of His creation might be able to see Him in His unfathomable love and immeasurable humility.

Chapter 6

God's love in the suffering and Crucifixion of His Son

"... He humbled himself, and became obedient unto death, even the death of the cross."
Phil. 2:8

The redeeming crucifixion of our Lord and Savior Jesus Christ is not simply a result of contemporary circumstances, but providential event that manifested the evil of mankind and the immeasurable love of God. The Lord Jesus Christ started His ministry at a time when man's descent into a state of corruption was at its worst. This was manifest in the failure of the Pharisees, the Scribes, and the priests to see the truth that was in front of their eyes. They were blinded by extreme hatred. Hate is the opposite of love. Therefore, someone with a hateful heart cannot see and understand the love of God. The Lord Jesus Christ said, *"seeing they see not..." /Matt. 13:13/,* speaking about those who were blinded with hatred.

Therefore, to manifest His love that surpasses any measure of human intellect and understanding, He came to give His life for us at a time when man's hatred for what is good was extreme. He wanted to show us the power of His love, by submitting Himself to suffering by the evil deeds of men. So, it was not by chance, but by His providential wisdom that He suffered and died on the Cross.

I. His death on the Cross

"For when we were yet without strength, in due time Christ died for the ungodly... God commends His love toward us, in that while we were yet sinners, Christ died for us."
Rom. 5:5-8

True love is not reflected in reciprocating someone's love, but in loving those who hate. The Lord Jesus Christ taught, *"If you love them who love you, what reward have you? do not even the tax collectors do the same?"* /Matt. 5:46/. So, the Lord Jesus Christ wanted to show us what true love is like. Speaking about His crucifixion hundreds of years before it happened, the Lord God said, *"I have spread out my hands all day unto a rebellious people, who walk in a way that was not good, after their own thoughts."* /Is. 65:2/. At the very site where Adam's remains were laid, He was crucified with His hands stretched out and nailed on the Cross.

In hatred they have nailed his hands on the Cross, but in love, He stretched out His hands to call all the children of Adam, including His crucifiers, so that all may have life in Him. Yearning for mankind to come to Him and drink from the fountain of love, He said I thirst in love, but they gave Him a mixture of bitter gall and vinegar in hatred. In His infinite love, He walked in the Garden of Eden coming to Adam and asked, *"Where ae you?"* In hatred they nailed His feet on the Cross. In hatred they screamed *"crucify Him,"* In love, He prayed, *"Father, forgive them for they know not what they are doing."* The righteous judge was judged by sinners. The Lord who created the world by His word, was now silent in front of His accusers. The prophet Isaiah marveled at His silence saying, *"He was oppressed, and He was afflicted, yet He opened not His mouth: He is brought as a lamb to the slaughter, and as a sheep before her shearers is dumb, so He opened not his mouth." /Is. 53:7/.*

In His silence is manifested the power of His love. Who would stand silent, when falsely accused? Who, having the power to destroy, would be restrained from destroying His accusers? Isn't that why the chief priest and the Scribes mocked him saying, *"He saved others; Himself he cannot save. If He be the King of Israel, let Him now come down from the cross, and we will believe Him. He trusted in God; let him deliver Him now, if He will have Him: for He said, I am the Son of God."?* Why didn't He do what they were daring Him to do, so that they would believe in Him? The simple answer is, He had already done that, and they still did not believe in Him. And He would do more in His infinite love so that they could open and see the truth, but they still would not believe in Him.

He kept silent and had to suffer for our sake, because it had to be so, for the sake of our redemption. The Lord Jesus Christ said, there is no greater love than giving one's life for another. And He did exactly that for our sake:

"Surely, He has borne our griefs, and carried our sorrows: yet we did esteem Him stricken, smitten by God, and afflicted. But He was wounded for our transgressions, He was bruised for our iniquities: the chastisement of our peace was upon Him; and with His stripes we are healed. All we like sheep have gone astray; we have turned everyone to his own way; and the Lord has laid on Him the iniquity of us all." /Is. 53:4-6/

His death on the Cross is much more than just giving "one's life for another." He had to die for our sake, so that we may have life in Him. But why suffer? Why on the Cross? That is because He wanted to heal every sense of our body that led to the fall of Adam and Eve. He saw the worst of man's sinful deeds to heal the eyes that looked at the forbidden fruit with a sinful desire. He heard the mockery and insults of the people to heal the ears that heard the counsel of the devil. His feet were nailed on the Cross to heal the feet that chose the sinful path to the forbidden fruit. He was nailed on the cross to heal the hands that took what was not allowed. He drank a mixture of gall and vinegar to heal the mouth that tasted the forbidden fruit and brought death and destruction upon us.

His death was not a simple death. Our Lord and Savior Jesus Christ paid with every sense of His body to heal every sense of our body that was corrupted and wounded because of sin. Man rebelled against God with a desire to be like Him. The Son of God humbled himself and partook our nature so that He can be like us and pay for our transgressions. That is why the Prophet Isaiah said, *"The Lord has laid on Him the iniquity of us all."* /Is. 53:6/

It is also important everyone believe that He truly suffered and died. Because man could not understand His love in His benevolence, He came to show His love in the ultimate act of giving His life for us. *"For God so loved the world, that He gave His only begotten Son, that whoever believes in Him should not perish but have everlasting life."* /John 3:17/. In this manner of death, death on the cross, everyone would know that He had indeed died at their hands. Because He was silent when they accused Him, and looked weak when they crucified Him, they believed that His death would be the end of Him. St. Paul wrote, *"The preaching of the Cross is to them that perish foolishness, but unto us which are saved, it is the power of God."* /1 Cor. 1:18/. This power that was manifested on the Cross was not the power of God's wrath to destroy His enemies, but rather the power of His love to save the world. That is why He died on the cross, so that the power of His love for mankind, despite their sinfulness, may be manifest.

The Lord Jesus Christ spoke of His crucifixion as a moment of Glory: *"The hour is come, that the Son of man should be glorified."/John 12:23/*. That is because the power of His love is glorious over all deeds of evil since the fall of man. It was because of His love manifested on the cross, that many including the gentiles would glorify Him. An Eastern Orthodox priest, Michael Pomaznsky, captures God's manifestation of His love in his suffering and death in these beautiful words: *"There is no measuring-stick for the all-surpassing wealth of God 's love, manifest in His mercy for the fallen and for sinners in miracles, in healings, and finally, in His innocent sacrificial death, with prayer for His crucifiers."*[14]

But what His enemies failed to see in His suffering and death, He would give them an opportunity to see in His resurrection.

II. His Resurrection

The Lord Jesus Christ did many wonders and signs before His crucifixion, that the world may know Him by His works. He was even telling the scribes and the pharisees that what they were witnessing in Him was what was written about Him in the scriptures. When He came to Jerusalem for the last time before His crucifixion, many people including children received Him, singing *"Hossana to the Son of David, blessed is He who comes in the name of the Lord." /Matt.*

---

[14] Pomazansky, M. (1985, October 1). Orthodox Dogmatic Theology.

21:9/. But the chief priests and the Scribes were not happy and asked why He did not rebuke the children. Reminding them that they were witnessing the fulfillment of a prophecy by King David, He said, *"Have you not read out of the mouth of babes and sucklings, you have perfected praise?" /Matt 21:9; Psalm 8:2/.*

Immediately after coming into Jerusalem, the Lord Jesus Christ went into the Temple and found people trading money and merchandize. He drove all those trading in the Temple and threw their tables. And He said to them, *"It is written My house shall be made a house of prayer, but you have made it a den of thieves." /Matt. 21:13/.* The disciples remembered that this was the fulfillment of what was written by King David: *"The zeal of Your house has eaten me up." /John 69:9; John 2:17/.* But the chief priests and the Scribes sought to find ways to destroy Him. This was yet another opportunity for them to see that they were witnessing a prophecy being fulfilled.

Instead of inclining their hearts to the truth that was unfolding before them, they always sought to find ways to discredit or deny the Lord Jesus Christ. In the Gospel of John, on Chapter 9, there is a story about a man who was born blind. The disciples asked the Lord Jesus Christ if this man was born blind because of his or his parents' sins. He answered them that it was not because of his or his parents' sins, but that the glory of God might be revealed. He mixed His

As I have Loved You

saliva with soil to make mud, rubbed the blind man's eyes with it and told him to go and wash in the pool of Siloam. The blind man did as he was told, and he came back seeing.

But instead of seeing the glory of God, many started doubting that this man was the same person they had seen begging. They even doubted that he had been born blind in the first place. So, they asked his parents and himself if he had been born blind. He told them that He was the same person that was born blind. He was brought in front of the Pharisees for questioning. He told them the truth again and asked them if they wanted to be His disciples too. But they said *"We are the disciples of Moses. We know that God spoke to Moses, as for this Man (Jesus Christ), we do not know where He comes from."* The man marveled at the stiff hardness of their heart and said to them, *"Why , this is amazing thing! You do not know where He comes from, and yet He opened my eyes. We know that God does not listen to sinners, but if anyone is a worshiper of God and does His will, God listens to Him. Never since the world began has it been heard that anyone opened the eyes of a man born blind."* The Pharisees were upset that He tried to reason with them, and they cast him out of the synagogue.

Because of such tendency they have had to make excuses and deny the truth, the Lord Jesus did everything so that they would have no plausible excuse for denying the truth. As He was crucified in plain sight, on the Cross and died at their hands, the events that followed until His resurrection happened in a way that they would have plenty of opportunity to see the truth and the love of God.

After His crucifixion, the Lord Jesus Christ was buried in a new tomb. The Israelites had a tradition of laying the departed with the remains of their forefathers. But the Lord Jesus Christ was buried in a new tomb which Joseph of Arimathea prepared for himself: *"And when Joseph had taken the body, he wrapped it in a clean linen cloth, and laid it in his own new tomb…" /Mat. 27:59/*. This happened in God's infinite wisdom not to give any reason for anyone to deny His resurrection by His own authority. It is written in 2Kings 13:21 that a man was raised from the dead when his body touched the bones of the prophet Elisha. If the Lord Jesus Christ was buried next to one of the prophets, His doubters might have reasoned that He was risen because of the prophet. But to prevent such doubters of any reason to deny His resurrection, He was buried in a new tomb, where no one was laid in before Him.[15]

After Jesus body was placed in the tomb, the chief priests and the Pharisees came to Pontius Pilate and said, *"Sir, we remember that this deceiver said, while He was yet alive, after three days I will rise*

---

[15] MKUSA Education and Apostolate Service Section, 2016

again. Command therefore that the sepulcher be made sure until the third day, lest His disciples come by night, and steal Him away, and say unto the people, He is risen from the dead: so, the last error shall be worse than the first." /Matt. 27:62-64/. But Pontius Pilate told them to seal the tomb and to put their own guards.

In his commentary about why this happened, St. John Chrysostom said: *"So that if the sepulcher be sealed, there will be no unfair dealing. For there could not be. So, then the proof of His resurrection has become incontrovertible by what you have put forward. For because it was sealed, there was no unfair dealing. But if there was no unfair dealing, and the sepulcher was found empty, it is manifest that He is risen, plainly and incontrovertibly. Do you see, how even against their will they contend for the proof of the truth?"*[16] We have seen how the Lord God deals with us fairly in the tree of knowledge as a symbol of fairness. St John Chrysostom also here details why the Lord allowed for His crucifiers to put their own guards so that there would be no "unfair dealing." Who can accuse the Lord of anything He would wish to do? But, because of His infinite love, He always deals with us fairly for our own benefit:

---

[16] John Chrysostom on Matthew 27:63 - Catena Bible & Commentaries. (n.d.). Catena Bible & Commentaries. https://catenabible.com/com/57eb0db7b0d44ee10cfac616

"He will judge the world with righteousness, and the people with fairness." /Psalm 98:9/

In saying, *"the last error shall be worse than the first,"* They were inadvertently speaking about themselves. Because their denial of what they themselves witnessed was worse than all that they had done before, including crucifying the Lord Jesus Christ. St. John Chrysostom said, *"against their will they contend for the proof of the truth."* Indeed, against their will, but it was according to the will of God, and moreover about His love. Even though they afflicted and crucified Him, He would give them another chance to see the truth and believe in Him, so that they would be saved. He already showed them how merciful He is even when He was on the cross, replying to what the criminal on His right asked.

The criminal on the right side of the Lord Jesus Christ on the cross asked Him, *"Lord, remember me when you come in Your kingdom."* And the Lord replied, *"Verily I say unto you, today shall you be with Me in paradise." /Luke 23:42-43/.* A criminal, who by his own admission deserved to suffer on the cross, asked the Lord Jesus Christ to remember him, not in the moment, but when He comes again for judgement. The criminal on the on the left of the Lord Jesus Christ, with no sense of remorse for his criminal acts, joined the mockery of the Lord's crucifiers and said, *"If You are Christ, save yourself and us." /Luke 23:39/.* But the criminal on the right did not ask *"If you are the Christ, remember me in your kingdom."* But He called Him "Lord." Therefore, he believed that Christ was indeed the Lord, the Son of God, who could save him in that very moment. He knew that the Lord was innocent, but endured affliction and suffering on the cross willingly. He knew that the Lord was doing all this because of His unconditional love to redeem mankind. He knew that He was witnessing an unparalleled act of love. But He also knew that he did not deserve forgiveness for what He had done. So, instead of asking to be saved in that moment, He asked, penitently, for the Lord Jesus Christ to remember him on judgment day. But the love of God manifests to the repentant in the very moment a sinner repents and returns to Him. So, He said *"today you shall be with Me in paradise."*

A criminal condemned to die on the cross became the first of the children of Adam to enter paradise. He who was judged to die because of his crimes, now received mercy at the very moment of his repentance and he heard the words of salvation. He asked to be spared by the love of God on judgment day, but the love of God is not distant. It is a present reality for the sinner who truly repents. It is in recognition of this unparalleled love that we pray in the same words of this criminal in the Divine Liturgy, saying *"Remember us Lord in Your Kingdom."*

This was an opportunity for those who crucified the Lord, to think about His mercifulness and love, when they finally come to learn of the Lord's resurrection - so they would repent and seek His loving mercy, knowing that despite what they had done to Him, He would forgive them. It is for the same reason, He prayed for them saying, *"Father, forgive them for they know not what they are doing." /Luke 23:34/*

The guards, the chief priests and the scribes selected to keep watch on the tomb, were the first witnesses of the moments immediately after the resurrection of the Lord Jesus Christ. He was risen from the dead without the need to unwrap the linen with which His body was wrapped, and without opening the Tomb. Immediately after He was risen, *"there was a great earthquake: for the angel of the Lord descended from heaven and came and rolled back the stone from the door and sat upon it. His countenance was like lightning, and his clothing white as snow: And for fear of him the guards did shake and became as dead men." /Matt. 28:2-4/.* The guards immediately went into the city and testified of what they had seen to the chief priests. This happened so that His crucifiers would have a firsthand testimony of the truth regarding the resurrection of the Lord Jesus Christ. They were mystically compelled to seal the tomb and to put their own guards to watch it.

This was an opportunity for them to learn that they have crucified not just an innocent man, but their

Savior. And recalling how He prayed for them on the cross saying, *"Lord, forgive them for they know not what they are doing,"* and remembering how He promised the criminal on His right-side salvation, they could have simply repented and benefit from the redeeming love of Jesus Christ. But, after counseling with the elders, they bribed the guards and told them to say, *"Say this, His disciples came by night, and stole him away while we slept."* /Matt. 28:13/. In His abundant love, the Lord did not leave His crucifiers without the testimony of His resurrection by the guards they entrusted at the tomb, but God's love can't be understood with a heart full of hatred.

III. His Ascension

The ascension of the Lord Jesus Christ is yet another manifestation of God's love. It shows how much He glorified man that was condemned to death and corruption.

As His birth, His baptism, His Crucifixion and His Resurrection, the Ascension of the Lord Jesus Christ is also a significant event we find in prophecy: *"Who has ascended into heaven, or descended? Who has gathered the wind in His fists? Who has bound the waters in His garment? Who has established all the ends of the earth? What is His name, and what is Son's name?"* /Prov. 30:4/

We find the account of the Ascension of the Lord Jesus Christ in the Gospel of Mark 19, Luke 24, and in the first chapter of the Book of Acts. It is also one of the teachings besides Baptism Jesus Christ revealed to Nicodemus: *"No man has ascended up to heaven, but He that came down from heaven, even the Son of man which is in heaven." /John 3:13/*

What we understand from these words of the Lord Jesus Christ is that, when we speak of the ascension of Jesus Christ, it is about His ascension in the flesh. Even though He descended from heaven and was incarnate from the Virgin Mary, He descended without being removed from his heavenly throne. That is why the Lord Jesus Christ said, *"... He came down from heaven, even the Son of man which is in heaven."*

To understand the significance of the Ascension, it is essential to look at the fall of Adam and Eve. Satan, disguised in the serpent said to Eve, *"You shall not surely die, for God knows that in the day you eat thereof (from the forbidden fruit), then your eyes shall be opened, and you shall be as gods." /Gen. 3:4-5/*

Satan does not even know what we think let alone what God knows. The only thing he knows is deception: On the first day of creation, he deceived some among the angels when he claimed to be 'the creator." He fell from grace because of this deception. He, therefore, believed that he would cause the same fate for Adam & Eve if he could incline their thought to that of his deceptive thought – which is aspiring to be gods.

But what God knows, and the devil did not until the ascension of Jesus Christ – is that Adam and Eve could fall from grace but would be redeemed and truly be one with God. This was fulfilled through the incarnation of the Lord Jesus Christ when He became man from the Virgin Mary, and our nature was glorified by His ascension.

In His incarnation, the Divine, the Son of God, was made one with our humanity. In his Ascension, our body, which was condemned to death because of the devil's deception, has been ascended to heaven and sits at the right hand of God the Father. Yes, the Son of man came down from heaven to save us, because He *"desired to set Adam free, whose heart was sad and sorrowful, and to bring him back to his former place."*[17]

On the same night that He was crucified, St Peter testified in his first Epistle saying: *"... being put to death in the flesh, but quickened by the Spirit, by which He also went and preached unto the spirits in prison."* /1 Pet. 3:18-19/. Speaking of the glorification of our body, St Ephrem again on Thursday's Praise of Mary said: *"God dwelt in her womb, and became perfectly man, so that He might deliver Adam, and forgive him his sins, and make him dwell in heaven."*

---

[17] Monday's Wudassie Mariam by St. Ephrem the Syrian,

How wonderful it is that the Lord God rewarded mankind with the very deceptive words of Satan, with the very cause of our disobedience: Adam and Eve disobeyed the Lord God and ate the forbidden fruit because they wanted to be like God. But, through His loving grace, He united His divinity with our nature through the Virgin Mary. The reward of sin is death, but the reward of repentance is glory – for God is loving to glorify the repentant.

If the Lord God humbled Himself to become man & loved us unto death, how much more should we do for our own salvation and eternal glory so that we can be partakers of His redeeming sacrifice? We are not just given the promise of resurrection, but also the ascension to enter into His eternal glory.

St John the apostle testified of this immeasurable manifestation of God's love in these words: *"Behold, what manner of love the Father has bestowed upon us, that we should be called the children of God: therefore, the world knows us not, because it knew Him not. Beloved, now are we the children of God, and it does not yet appear what we shall be: but we know that, when He shall appear, we shall be like Him." /1 John 3:1 – 2/*

Chapter 7

God's Love in the Sacraments

Sacraments are visible spiritual rites through which we receive invisible grace or gifts of God. The invisible grace we receive through the sacraments are the means or the path by which we become partakers of God's kingdom. It is a gift freely given to all for our salvation through the redeeming sacrifice of our Lord and Savior Jesus Christ. It is only by faith that we become partakers of divine grace: *"We have peace with God through our Lord Jesus Christ, by whom also we have access by faith into this grace..." /Rom. 5:1-2/*. It is the means by which the love of God is revealed to us.

The ascension of the Lord Jesus Christ after His redeeming sacrifice and His resurrection was not the end of our relationship with Him, but the beginning of a newer relationship through the Sacraments by which we continue to receive and participate in His divine grace. That is why He promised the apostles saying, *"I am with you always, even unto the end of the world. Amen." /Matt 28:20/*.

I. Baptism

When Adam and Eve ate the forbidden fruit, they lost the grace of childhood and were exiled from paradise. They could no longer be partakers of God's divine glory. The Lord God therefore prepared a path for man to return to His former state and grow in the grace of God. For that, it was important for man to be adopted again as the child of God. It is through the Sacrament of Baptism that man is adopted again as the child of God, and no longer live in bondage to sin. Through baptism , we are born again into a new person with all the potential to partake of His divine glory once again. That is why baptism is the first sacrament administered to new believers since the apostolic era. *(Acts 2:41; 8:12; 8:36-38; 9:18; 18:18; 19:5).* It is a gift, freely given to us according to His love and mercy: *"Repent and be baptized every one of you in the name of Jesus Christ for the remission of sins, and you shall receive the gift of the Holy Ghost. /Acts 2:38 – 39/*

Through Baptism we become the children of God. *"You received the Spirit of adoption, whereby you cry Abba, Father." /Rom 8:15/.* And if we are the children of God, then we are also heirs to His Kingdom, which He prepared for us from the foundation of the world: *"Unless one is born again, He cannot see the Kingdom of God."/ John 3:3/*

Through baptism, we are called from the temporal exile in a land of sin and corruption, to an eternal joy and inheritance. Haran, the country of Abraham's family and relatives, was a symbol of this land of exile, and Canaan, the land the Lord God promised for Abrahm and his descendants, was a symbol of God's eternal kingdom. The promise to Abraham at the time was also a symbol of the promise for the inheritance of the eternal Kingdom under the new covenant – which starts with the adoption as the children of God through baptism. That is why St. Paul said, *"For as many of you as were baptized into Christ have put on Christ . . . And if you are Christ's, then you are Abraham's seed, and heirs according to the promise."* /Gal 3:27-29/

The words of St. Paul to the Galatians, *"For as many of you as were baptized into Christ have **put on Christ**..."* infer that through Baptism, not only are we adopted as children again, but also begin an intimate relationship with Him – the kind of intimate relationship Adam and Eve had with Him before the Fall. While we are unworthy sinners, God manifests His abundant love for us through the gift of Baptism – the first of the Sacraments. St. John emphasizes this manifestation of God's love, saying, *"Behold, what manner of love the Father has bestowed upon us, that we should be called the children of God"* /1 John 3:1/. St. John indicates that this intimacy is only the beginning of our growth in the grace of God and said that we are destined for greater glory: *"Beloved, now are we the children of God, and it does not yet appear* *what we shall be: but we know that, when he shall appear, we shall be like him." /1 John 3:2/.*

Through Baptism we also become partakers in the redeeming sacrifice and glorious resurrection of our Lord and Savior Jesus Christ: *"Do you not know that as many of us as were baptized into Christ Jesus were baptized into His death?"* /Romans 6:3/. *". . . Buried with Him in baptism, in which you also were raised with Him . . ."* /Colossians 2:12/. The contemplation of God's love in the grace of such glory and honor leads us into a sea of marvel we cannot swim out of!

The Lord Jesus Christ was incarnate, not just to redeem us from the bondage of sin, but also to set an example for us so that we can be partakers of His redeeming love and sacrifice. Unlike many that preach what they do not practice, He set examples for us in His deeds. To indicate to us that Baptism is the first Sacrament that we should receive to be adopted as children, He made His baptism the beginning of His ministry. He did not of course need to be baptized because He is the source and the giver of grace. But He was baptized to set an example for us, so that we know Baptism is the beginning of a life of discipleship. That is also why He commissioned the apostles with these words: *"Make disciples of all nations, baptizing them in the name of the Father, and of the Son and of the Holy Spirit."* /Matthew 28:19/

Our knowledge of God comes from His self-revelation. In creation, He revealed Himself to us in His love and the grandeur of His magnificent creation. In His baptism, the Holy Trinity in three persons was explicitly revealed – the Father spoke from the clouds saying, *"This is my beloved Son in Whom I am well pleased."* The Son was in the Jordan River being baptized by John the Baptist, and the Holy Spirit came upon Him in the form of a dove. /Matt. 3:16-17/. In the words of the Father, His love for mankind is manifested. He bears testimony of the Son, so that we know He is giving His only begotten, and beloved Son for our salvation. He said, *"... in Whom I am well pleased."* knowing that through the suffering and death of His Son, His crown of creation whom He created in His own image and likeness would be saved and alive again.

II. Confirmation

Confirmation is the sacrament through which we receive the seal of the Holy Spirit. This Sacrament is also known as the Sacrament of Holy Myron because it is administered by anointing with oil. Confirmation used to be imparted to the baptized by the laying on of hands: *"Then laid they (Peter & John) their hands on them, and they received the Holy Ghost."* /Acts 8:17/. When the number of believers started to grow outside of Jerusalem, the disciples could not go everywhere to lay their hands on the believers to impart the gift of the Holy Spirit. So, they started a rite of prayer over Holy Myron, which would be distributed so that this sacrament may be administered with anointing of this holy oil. Today, it is administered right after Baptism and before the Sacrament of Holy Communion.

The Lord God, *"who at sundry times and in diverse manners spoke in time-past unto the fathers by the prophets, hath in these last days spoken unto us by His Son"* /Heb. 1 : 1 – 2/. And we continue to partake of the love and grace of God through the Sacrament of Confirmation. St. John the apostle wrote, *"But you have an anointing from the Holy One."* /1 John 2:20/. *"The anointing which you have received from Him abides in you."* /1 John 2:27/. St. John's expression of this sacrament through anointing shows another intimate relationship we have with the Lord God.

Priests, kings, and instruments of worship in the Old Covenant used to be anointed with oil: *"You shall put them upon Aaron your brother, and his sons with him; and shall anoint them, and consecrate them, and sanctify them, that they may minister unto me in the priest's office."* /Ex. 28:41; 29:7/; *"And you shalt take the anointing oil, and anoint the tabernacle and all that is therein, and shall hallow it and all the vessels thereof."* /Ex. 40:9/; *"Samuel took the horn of oil and anointed him in the midst of his brothers; and the Spirit of the Lord came upon David from that day forward."* /1 Sam. 16:13/. But the anointing with Holy Myron was different. It is an anointing of the Holy Spirit, which abides in us, lives in us. St. Paul calls it an anointing by which we are *"sealed for the day of redemption."* /Ephesians 4:30/. His words show us that this is a redeeming sacrament, which shows the continuous love and care of the Lord God – a love manifested by the seal of the Holy Spirit for the day of redemption or judgment day.

The fact that this sacrament was administered by the laying on of hands at first, and later with anointing, is a rite that marks an intimate expression of love. The Lord who created us with His hands, instituted this sacrament with a redeeming rite of administration through the hands of the apostles.

III. Holy Communion

The love of God in this sacrament is manifest in the words the Lord Jesus Christ spoke to the apostles on the night of the institution of this Sacrament – on the night of the "Last Supper. *"Jesus took bread, and blessed it, and broke it, and gave it to the disciples, and said, Take, eat; this is my body. And he took the cup, and gave thanks, and gave it to them, saying, drink you all of it; For this is my blood of the new covenant, which is shed for many for the remission of sins. /Matt. 26:25-28/*

He, who in His essence is a consuming fire, has given us His body and His blood for our consumption so that we can have communion with Him. The timing of the institution of this Sacrament is a profound act of love – in the same night that He was betrayed, He gave us His redeeming body and blood, so that by His suffering, sacrifice, shedding His blood and by His death, we might be alive. What manner of love is this that on the night His enemies prepared to take Him captive and crucify Him, He prepared a sacrifice to free them from the bondage of sin. On the night Judas betrayed Him, He allowed Him to partake of this Divine Mystery of love. He did this so that Judas would not feel to have been left out of this moment and would not give an excuse for not repenting. He instituted this sacrament, knowing that all his apostles would soon leave Him: *"Then all the disciples forsook him, and fled." /Matt. 26:56/.*

This divine mystery is celebrated in the Divine Liturgy – which is an angelic worship conducted in the manner of heavenly worship. In the Divine Liturgy, we stand in the presence of God in the same manner angels stand in front of the throne of God. Yet, our participation in this angelic worship transcends even that of angels in heaven because we partake of His body and blood – which is a consuming fire, but we are not consumed by it. The sacrifice of the Old Testament was consumed by fire, but the redeeming sacrifice of the New Testament is itself a consuming fire. Yet, because of His grace and love, we partake of it for our salvation. These words in the Anaphora of the Virgin Mary speak of the love of God manifested in this mystery: *"He is mighty that is unfathomable; but He became humble among us. He is the most high, to whom none can attain, but among us He took upon Him the form of a servant. He is the impalpable fire, but we saw Him and felt Him and ate and drank with Him."/88/.*

In the Sacrament of Confirmation, we have seen that the anointing – which is the seal of the Holy Spirit - abides in us */1 John 2:27/.* Through Holy Communion, we abide in Christ and He abides in us: *"He who eats My flesh and drinks my body, abides in Me and I in Him." /John 6:56/.* In this divine mystery, we enter into a communion with our Lord and Savior Jesus Christ, we all become one: *"The cup of blessing which we bless, is it not the communion of the blood of Christ? The bread which we break, is it not the communion of the body of Christ? For we, though many, are one bread and one body; for we all partake of that one bread." /1 Corinthians 10:16-18/.* It is because of this unspeakable manifestation of love that we say in the Divine Liturgy, we are accorded more than the angels, not according to our deeds, but according to His love and mercy.

In the Divine Liturgy, we experience a presence with the apostles at the institution of this sacrament, and at the same time, experience the eternal kingdom where we stand in the presence of the Father, the Son, and the Holy Spirit. As we grow in faith and the knowledge of the love of God, we experience greater favor - the joy of the kingdom God has prepared for the righteous. Therefore, in the rite of administration of this sacrament, not only do we hope for the eternal inheritance of His kingdom, but we get to experience a little bit of the same kingdom.

IV. Priesthood

This is a Sacrament through which a person receives the authority and the gift to minster unto God, to administer the Sacraments and to absolve or hold the sins of others. The Lord Jesus Christ is the source of the priesthood of the New Testament who appointed the apostles to minister unto Him. *"... a high priest was fitting for us, who is holy, harmless, undefiled, separate from sinners and has become higher than the heavens." /Heb 7:26/.* The high Priest, who is higher than the heavens is the incarnate Son of God, our Lord, and Savior Jesus Christ. St. Paul said "fitting" because there was none that is fitting to fulfill our salvation, through righteousness, self-sacrifice, or any deeds of virtue. Only the Son of God, the High Priest, who is holy, harmless, and undefiled could recreate man from a state of continual descent into corruption and destruction. Our salvation required not just the perfect Sacrifice, but also one who is fitting to offer the Sacrifice. He is the High Priest who offered Himself and redeemed us.

Priesthood is a calling for a Divine ministry (John 15:19)– because divine grace to minister unto God is imparted unto the person receiving it, and it also bestows the authority to impart the divine grace through the other sacraments. It is simply because of his loving grace that the Lord Jesus Christ gave to mankind the authority to minister unto Him in the heavenly image of angelic worship. Yet again, there is something greater bestowed upon those called into this divine ministry – the authority to absolve or hold the sins of many. This is a divine authority that He bestowed upon man.

The Jews accused the Lord Jesus Christ of blasphemy because of what He had said to those who came to Him for healing. On one occasion, when some people brought a paralytic man to Him for healing, the Lord Jesus Christ said to the paralytic, *"Your sins are forgiven."* But the Scribes and the Pharisees said, *"Who is this who speaks blasphemies? Who can forgive sins, but God alone?"* /Luke 5:20 – 21/

They were right in that this was a divine attribute. But they failed to see Him, despite many signs and wonders He did among them. And what is truly remarkable to imagine is that it is this divine attribute He bestowed upon mankind by His grace. He granted the apostles this authority saying to them: *"Verily I say unto you, whatsoever you shall bind on earth shall be what has been bound in heaven: and whatsoever you shall loose on earth shall be what has been loosed in heaven." /Matt 18:18/*. He said this to them before His crucifixion and affirmed it again after His resurrection: *"And when he had said this, he breathed on them, and said unto them, receive you the Holy Spirit: Whosoever's sins you remit, they are remitted unto them; and whosoever's sins you retain, they are retained. /John 20:22 – 23/*. The priesthood of the New Covenant is a gift by which we can marvel and appreciate the love of God, because this is an attribute of Godhead that He gave to the apostles and to their successors.

As He breathed on the apostles and said to them *"Receive the Holy Spirit"*, His apostles were given this authority to impart the Holy Spirit, so that those who believe may also receive the Holy Spirit through them: *"when they (St. Peter & St. John) were come down, prayed for them, that they might receive the Holy Spirit." /Acts 8:15/*.

We can see how profoundly different the priesthood of the New Covenant is from that of the Old Covenant. Under the Old covenant, the priests offered grain or animal sacrifice. This was not considered a real sacrifice, because it was offered only for a temporary atonement of sin. It was only a symbol of the true redeeming sacrifice, which is the Lord Jesus Christ Himself – which is offered by the priests of the New Covenant. Therefore, under the Old Covenant, the authority of the priest was limited as for an earthly ministry. But the priesthood of the New Covenant is for a divine ministry, for the new Lamb of the New Covenant, the Lord Jesus Christ, who was sacrificed once for all on the cross, is offered for an everlasting atonement of sin.

Now that He was fulfilling the Old Covenant and establishing a new covenant – not just for the Israelites, but for the world, He did not choose the apostles of the New Covenant from just the Levites, but from all the tribes of Israel. And He did not choose them from those considered elites of the society, but from those considered regular or lowly: *"For you see your calling, brethren, how that not many wise men after the flesh, not many mighty, not many noble, are called: But God has chosen the foolish things of the world to confound the wise; and God has chosen the weak things of the world to confound the things which are mighty"* /1 Cor. 26-27/. Priesthood therefore is a calling for a divine ministry – for the glory of God: See how God manifests His love, not just in establishing the priesthood of the New Covenant but bestowing divine attribute upon those not considered elites, educated, or righteous by society. When St. Paul said, *"... I am not meet to be an apostle, because I persecuted the Church of God,"* he is revealing the extraordinary love of God to receive such a calling despite his past deeds. */1 Cor. 15:9/*. The priesthood of the New Covenant is no longer a matter of birthright, as that of the Old Covenant, but a gift of divine attribute for a divine ministry, according to the love and beneficence of God. And He established this sacrament with the twelve apostles – men of no reputation in their society, but who would ultimately follow Him, in love, unto death – except one, Judas of Iscariot.

V.   Repentance (Confession)

God's love is the cause of our existence. His love is the cause of our livelihood. His love is the cause of His incarnation, suffering and death on the cross for our salvation. And if we fall in sin, God's love is the basis for the sacrament of confession & repentance. The prophet Joel said, *"...Return to the Lord your God, For He is gracious and compassionate..."* */Joel 2:13/*. These words show us that when we return to Him, we do so, not with a doubtful thought whether He would forgive us and accept us, but having an assurance that God will accept us and forgive our trespasses. That is why the apostle John wrote: *""If we confess our sins, He is faithful and just to forgive us our sins, and to cleanse us from all unrighteousness."* /1 John 1:9/.

The Lord Jesus Christ did not despise and turn away from those, considered sinful by society, during His ministry on earth. For that reason, the pharisees accused Him of eating with and going into the houses of sinners and tax collectors. But the Lord Jesus Christ said, *"I came not to call the righteous, but sinners to repentance."* /Luke 5:32/. We can see the love of God for all sinners in these words of the prophet Isaiah: *"Let the wicked forsake his way and the unrighteous man his thoughts; And let him return to the LORD, And He will have compassion on him, and to our God, For He will abundantly pardon."* /Is. 55:7/

This is a sacrament through which one receives absolution from His/her sins after repentance, and confession of his/her sins before a priest. Jesus Christ gave the disciples the authority to hold or absolve the sins of others /Matt. 18:18; John 20:23/. Accordingly, all sins have to be confessed before a priest for absolution: *"Unless you repent you will all likewise perish."* /Luke 13:5/. *"He who covers his sins will not prosper, but whoever confesses and forsakes them will have mercy"*

/Prov.28: 13/. Confession was practiced under the Old Covenant as we can see in these words: *"And it shall be, when he is guilty in any of these matters, that he shall confess that he has sinned in that thing; and he shall bring his trespass offering to the Lord for his sin which he has sinned"* */Lev.5: 5-6/*. Those who came to John the Baptist to be baptized used to confess before being baptized: *"Jerusalem, all Judea, and all the region around the Jordan went out to him and were baptized by him in the Jordan, confessing their sins"* */Matt.3: 566/*. The Lord Jesus Christ reaffirmed the continuity of this practice by sending those He healed to go to a priest for confession: *"Show yourself to the priest and offer the gift that Moses Commanded."* */Matt. 8:4/*

The loving care of the Lord God is apparent in the benefit of confessing before a priest. The priest gives free counsel, and is a guide, a confidante, and a companion in the journey to salvation. The prayer of absolution for the repentant believer gives the sinner a feeling unique to each individual. What manner of love did the criminal who was on the right side of the crucified Lord feel when he heard the words, *"today you will be with me in paradise?"* There is a great feeling of love, one feels in the prayer of absolution after confession and repentance. According to the assurance we have in the promise for the repentant sinner, we feel God's loving mercifulness in the words of absolution:

"May the Lord God absolve you of all your transgressions you have committed, knowingly and unknowingly…" This is a practice of repentance given to us, so that we feel the love and compassion of our Lord and Savior Jesus Christ – through the divine ministry He gave to His apostles.

In the gospel of Luke, on chapter 7, there is an interesting story about a woman who was a sinner that came into the house of a man named Simon where Jesus was dining in. She brought a perfume and started washing his feet with it, and drying his feet with her hair, crying all the while. Simon was a Pharisee who considered any association with a sinner a defilement. When he saw what the woman was doing, he reasoned in his mind that if Jesus was a prophet, He would have known that this woman was a sinner. But Jesus knew what he was thinking and told him the following story: *"There was a certain creditor who had two debtors: the one owed five hundred pence, and the other fifty. And when they had nothing to pay, he frankly forgave them both."* Then the Lord Jesus asked him, *"Tell me therefore, which of them will love him most?"* Simone replied, *"I suppose he, to whom he forgave the most."* The Lord Jesus said to him, *"you have rightly judged… Her sins, which are many, are forgiven; for she loved much: but to whom little is forgiven, the same loves little."*

Confession is a Sacrament of repentance where sinners experience the immeasurable love of God and love the more according to how much they are forgiven. It is a sacrament where a sinner gets a chance to fall at the feet of the Lord and feel the outpouring love of God. In this sacrament of love, the repentant sinner experiences the reality of the promise, *"He is faithful and just to forgive us our sins."* This is a sacrament in which we hear the loving voice of the Lord God when He called Adam out of His hiding: *"Where are you?"* It is the means by which we answer, *"here I am a sinner."*

This affectionate voice of God is not like the voice of one looking for a criminal – but the voice of one looking for a sinner, to restore him/her to righteousness. That is why St. Ephrem wrote this in His praise to the Virgin Mary: *"The Lord God loved to set Adam free, whose heart was sad and sorrowful, and to bring him back to his former place."* /Monday's Praise of Mary by St. Ephrem the Syrian./

VI. Matrimony

As we have seen in creation, one of the ways by which God's love is manifested for mankind is in the way He created Adam and Eve. He created them as one, and not separately as male and female like other creatures. The love of God in this manner of creating man and woman is manifest in the words

Adam spoke when he first saw Eve: *"This is now bone of my bones, and flesh of my flesh: she shall be called Woman, because she was taken out of Man." /Gen. 2:23/*. We see that the loving intimacy of a man and a woman does not come from any external force of attraction, but from the fact that they are created as one. And explaining the love of God that is therefore reflected in marriage, St. Paul said *"For no man ever yet hated his own flesh; but nourishes and cherishes it." /Eph. 5:29/*.

The invisible grace received through the sacrament of Holy Matrimony is this union of a man and a woman in the very same sense that Adam and Eve are one flesh. Affirming this mystery, the Lord Jesus Christ said, *"Therefore they are no more two, but one flesh. What therefore God has joined together, let not man put asunder." /Matt. 19:6/*.

Marriage is a spiritual institution in which God's love can be mirrored or reflected. St. Paul said, *"Wives, submit yourselves unto your own husbands, as unto the Lord. For the husband is the head of the wife, even as Christ is the head of the church: and he is the savior of the body. Therefore, as the church is subject unto Christ, so let the wives be to their own husbands in everything. Husbands, love your wives, even as Christ also loved the church, and gave himself for it." /Eph. 5:22-25/*. The Lord Jesus Christ said that there is no greater love than giving one's life for another. And according to what St. Paul said, this is the kind of love that is to be reflected in marriage – following the example of Christ. There is nothing greater than a life of harmony in marriage, loving parents want for their children. And such life is only possible if there is true love between the husband and the woman. According to His unconditional love, which is the kind of love the Lord God wanted to flourish in the first marriage between Adam and Eve, we are given the same grace in the Holy Matrimony of a man and a woman.

VII.   Unction of the Sick

This is a sacrament through which one is healed of physical and spiritual ailment. When our Lord Jesus Christ sent the disciples into the world, this was one of the sacraments they administered to the faithful: *"They went out and preached that people should repent. And they cast out many demons, and anointed with oil many who were sick, and healed them." /Mark 6:12/. "So, Jesus had compassion on them, and touched their eyes, and immediately their eyes received sight..." /Matt. 20:34/*

Many used to come to the Lord Jesus Christ for healing from different ailments. And He healed all that came to Him, with compassion and love: *"And Jesus went forth and saw a great multitude and was moved with compassion toward them and He healed their sick." /Matt. 14:14/.* He gave us this sacrament through the apostles so that His love continues to be manifest until He comes for judgement. *"And when he had called unto him his twelve disciples, he gave them power against unclean spirits, to cast them out, and to heal all manner of sickness and all manner of disease." /Matt 10:1/*

As the other sacraments, this is administered to the faithful: *"Is anyone among you sick? Let him call for the elders of the church, and let them pray over him, anointing him with oil in the name of the Lord. And the prayer of faith will save the sick, and the Lord will raise him up. And if he has committed sins, he will be forgiven." /James 5:14-15/.*

The healing here may not be necessarily of the flesh or the mind, but of the soul. If it is the will of God that the ailment is for transition into the next life, certainly *"the prayer of the faith will save the sick"* in his soul so that He will stand with the righteous on the right of the Lord Jesus Christ when He comes again in glory to judge the living and the dead.

Chapter 8

God's love in His Teachings

Among the longest teachings of the Lord in the gospel is the one recorded first in the Gospel of Matthew – The Sermon on the Mount – which is covered in four chapters. The central message in this sermon is love and other virtuous deeds that are constituents of love.

Christ's teaching was radical and unlike any teaching mankind had known before. He started His teaching with what are known as "The Beatitudes." He said *Blessed are the poor in spirit... they that mourn... the meek... those which hunger and thirst for the sake of righteousness... Blessed are you when they revile you and persecute you and shall say all manner of evil against you falsely, for my sake."* He reminded them the same happened to the prophets before them. At the end of the chapter /Matt 5/, He gave them a commandment that gave a new dimension to what love is: *"Love your enemies, bless them that curse you, do good to them that hate you, and pray for them who despitefully use you, and persecute you." /Matt. 5:44/.*

He went high up on a mountain to teach them this. Because what He taught them from a high place on a mountain in words, He would later teach them in His crucifixion – raised up on the Cross at Golgotha. The God who created us in His image and likeness, wants us to be like Him in works of love and righteousness. He said to love in the same manner that He loved us, *"that you may be the children of your Father in heaven... be ye therefore perfect, even as your Father which is in heaven is perfect."* /Matt. 5:45 – 48/.

Such love is the central message of Christ's teachings. That is why, as He taught them in words in his sermon on the mount, he would show his apostles how to humble oneself in such love, by washing their feet on the night of the Last Supper. Then He said to them, *"Know you what I have done to you? You call me Teacher and Lord: and you say rightly; for so I am. If I then, your Lord and Teacher, have washed your feet; you also ought to wash one another's feet. For I have given you an example, that you should do as I have done to you."* /John 13:12-15/. His humility though cannot be compared to the commandment He gave them. How can the humility of the Creator in washing the feet of the created be compared to the humility of mankind to each other? What is even remarkable is that He also washed the feet of Judas – knowing that He would betray Him the same night. How then is His humility comparable to mankind in practicing humility to one another? He was preparing them for a new commandment of love – the ultimate act of love manifested on the Cross.

Then He gave them a new commandment of love, saying *"A new commandment I give unto you, that you love one another;* **as I have loved you**, *that you also love one another." /John 13:34/*. In his commentary on this commandment, St. Cyril wrote: *"He plainly signifies the novelty involved in His command, and the extent by which the love that He enjoins surpasses that old idea of mutual love, by straightway adding the words: Even as I have loved you, that ye also love one another. We must investigate therefore the question how the Christ loved us, in order to understand clearly the full force of the words used... He humbled Himself, becoming obedient even unto death, yea, the death of the cross. And again: though He was rich, yet He became poor... Do you see the novelty of His love towards us? For whereas the Law /Deut. 6:5; Matt. 22:37/ enjoined the necessity of loving our brethren as ourselves... Marvelous then indeed was the extent of His love."*[18]

The first commandment, *"You shall love the Lord your God with all your heart, and with all your soul, and with all your mind." /Matt. 22:37/* is coupled with the commandment to the love of neighbor - not simply to love one another, but to love one another as Christ has loved us. That is why St. John wrote, *"Beloved, let us love one another: for love is of God;*

---

[18] Cyril of Alexandria on John 13:34 - Catena Bible & Commentaries. (n.d.). Catena Bible & Commentaries.

and everyone that loves, is born of God, and knows God. He that loves not knows not God; for God is love." /1st John 4:7-8/. The love of God, manifest in the Lord's teaching, is what gave his apostles the joy to suffer in His name.

Conclusion

God's love is the foundation of creation. Man was conceived in the mind of God, out of His desire to share His Divine glory and providence with Him. And the way to share in God's divine glory and providence is to share in His infinite and immeasurable love. That is why we find God's love to be a consistent theme throughout the Scripture, especially after the advent our Lord and Savior Jesus Christ. After He washed the feet of the disciples in humility, He said, *"A new commandment I give unto you, that you love one another; as I have loved you, that you also love one another."/John 13:34/*. But His love is not so simple to comprehend as the simplicity of the words.

His love for us has been constant since we were conceived in His divine plan of creation. As we have seen throughout the history of mankind since creation, there was no amount of our sin and transgression that would change His constant love for us. His love is not a consequence of conditions external to Himself. Despite our rebellion and vice, His constant love endures, because, as John the apostle said, God is love.

The very source of our tendency and ability to love is God Himself. It is the most important of all virtues we have, by the grace of God, so that we can be like Him. But we love according to conditions or forces external to us. If we love God, we do so because of His immeasurable love, His kindness, His mercifulness,

His protection... for us. Our love for others also depends on some conditions that are external to us. But God, simply loves. He also wants us to share in His divine love. So, He calls us not just to love others in favorable conditions, but as He has done, to simply love. That is why He said, *"You have heard that it has been said, You shall love your neighbor, and hate your enemy. But I say unto you, love your enemies, bless them that curse you, do good to them that hate you, and pray for them who despitefully use you, and persecute you."* /Matt. 5:43-44/

We were once alienated from God and enemies because of our works. So, loving one's enemy was acceptable. But now, that we are reconciled through the incarnation and the death of our Lord and Savior Jesus Christ, we are to resemble Him in His love. /Col. 1:21-22/. So, He said, love your enemies, and, right before He sacrificed Himself for us, who were enemies, He gave us the new commandment: to love one another as He has loved us. He loved us while we were sinners and enemies, and He said: *"love your enemies."* He prayed for those who crucified Him, and He said, *"bless those who curse you."* His hands were stretched out and nailed on the cross, stretched out in love to rebellious people, and He said: *"do good to them that hate you."* He prayed on the Cross for his crucifiers, and He said: *"pray for them who despitefully use you and persecute you."*

The words of the Lord Jesus Christ, right before Judas came with a band of officers from the chief priests and the Pharisees, are words that reveal the love accorded unto us by God in respect to the love within the Holy Trinity. Praying to the Father, He said *"... you have sent me, and have loved them, as you have loved me."* /John 17:23/. In these words, the Lord Jesus Christ is revealing to us that the love of God for us is no less than the inexplicable love that is one with the very essence of His being. Describing this marvel, St. Cyril wrote, *"Who showers, as it were, upon us the things that are His, and shares with His creatures what appertains to Himself alone."*[19]

His love is not just one that has the power to save us, but also the will to bestow this divine love in us, so that He may abide in us, and us in Him: *"... that the love with which you have loved me may be in them, and I in them."* /John 17:24/.

The central message of Jesus' disciples is also love. Not just their message in words and epistles, but also in deeds. For they have testified in His name, with joy for being persecuted for it, yet with love, that is a reflection of God's love for us. This is what we have seen in the first of the martyrs, St. Stephen. Standing accused of preaching in the name of Jesus Christ, he was not afraid to speak the truth. And while they were

---

[19] "Cyril of Alexandria on John 17:23." Catena Bible & Commentaries

stoning him, he simply kneeled and, *"cried with a loud voice, Lord, lay not this sin to their charge."* /Acts 7:60/.

We are called to resemble our Lord and Savior Jesus Christ. That is why St. Paul wrote, *"You are to imitate me, even as I imitate Christ."* /1 Cor. 11:1/. Commenting on this statement of St. Paul, St. John Chrysostom said, *"This is the rule of the most perfect Christianity, a landmark exactly laid down, the point that stands highest of all. Nothing can make a person like Christ more than caring for one's neighbors."* How blessed are those that lived and labored diligently to imitate Christ in their love?

It is when we understand the marvel and the novelty of God's love that we can fulfil His commandment:

As I have loved you, that you also love one another!
/John 13:34/

Made in the USA
Columbia, SC
08 July 2025